A ROADMAP TO RECOVERY

— OVERCOMING —

BINGE EATING

DISORDER

8 ACTIONABLE STRATEGIES
TO MANAGE TRIGGERS, REGAIN CONTROL
AND BOOST PHYSICAL & EMOTIONAL WELLNESS

AN INTERACTIVE WORKBOOK

ALLEN CROSS

CONTENTS

Introduction xi

Chapter 1: Understanding Binge Eating Disorder—Unveiling the Basics 1

What Is Binge Eating Disorder? 2

Journaling 3

What Causes BED? 4

    Perfectionism 4

    Dieting 4

    Mood Disorders 5

    Trauma 5

    Bullying 5

    Drug and Alcohol Use 6

    Genetics 6

    Obesity 6

Identifying Symptoms and Signs 7

    Stashing Food Away/Missing Food 7

    Social Isolation 8

    Finding Empty Food Packaging 8

    Loss of Control 8

    Feelings of Shame, Disgust, and Guilt After Eating 9

    Eating Not Triggered by Hunger 9

    Eating Rapidly 9

    Gastrointestinal Issues 10

Recognizing the Effects of BED 10

    Short-Term Effects 11

        Digestive Issues 11

Weight Gain 11

Trouble Sleeping 12

Long-Term Effects 12

Obesity 12

Heart Disease 13

Diabetes 13

Isolation 13

Chapter 2:   The Prevalence of Binge Eating Disorder—Knowing You're Not Alone 15

Statistics and Data on BED 16

Prevalence in Adults 16

Prevalence in Children and Teenagers 17

Health Effects 18

Treatment Statistics 19

Common Misconceptions and Stigmas Surrounding BED 19

BED Is Only a Problem in Overweight/Obese People 19

Children Can't Have BED 20

Going on a Diet Will Cure BED 20

Overeating and Binge Eating Are the Same 21

Men Don't Get BED 21

There Are No Long-Term Effects of BED 21

Understanding Co-Occurring Disorders 22

Workbook Activity: Reflection on Personal Experiences and Insights 23

Reflective Questions 24

Chapter 3:   The BED Cycle—Understanding the Vicious Cycle of Binge Eating 29

Restrictive Diets 29

The Pressure to Eat: Emotional and External Factors 31

The Aftermath: Shame and Self-Blame 33

Workbook Activity: Mapping Your BED Cycle 34

Chapter 4:   Introduction to BED Recovery 41

Can BED be Cured? 42

The Role of Professional Treatment 42

   Therapy 43

      Guided Self-Therapy 44

      Cognitive Behavioral Therapy (CBT) 44

      Dialectical Behavioral Therapy (DBT) 45

      Unguided Self-Therapy 46

      One-On-One Therapy 47

      Group Therapy 47

   Medication 48

   Nutrition Counseling 48

The Power of Self-Care 49

Workbook Activity: Strategy #1—Managing Your Expectations 49

   Step 1: Goal Identification 50

   Step 2: SMART Goal Setting 50

   Step 3: Clarify Your Goals 51

   Step 4: Action Plan 54

   Step 5: Commitment and Accountability 55

   Reflective Questions 56

**Chapter 5: Addressing Concerns—Overcoming Hurdles on the
Path to Recovery** 61

Strategy #2: Embracing a Growth Mindset 62

   Why is a Growth Mindset Important for Your Recovery? 62

      Allows You to Embrace Change 62

      Drives Lifelong Learning 63

      Inspires Positive Results 63

      Builds Resilience 64

      Helps You Learn From Mistakes 64

   How to Embrace a Growth Mindset 64

      Don't Identify Problems, Recognize Challenges 65

      Embrace the Good and Bad 65

      Practice Gratitude 66

      Don't Be Afraid to Ask for Help 66

      Set Goals 67

Be Curious and Try New Things..67

Learn From Failure 67

Don't Resent Criticism 68

Navigating Limited Support: Building a Network.....................................68

Benefits of a Social Support System 69

Increases Resilience 69

Better Overall Health 69

Provide Valuable Guidance 70

Enhance Wins and Decrease Losses.......................................70

Improved Mental Health 70

How to Build a Social Support System 71

Join a Support Group..71

Try Therapy 71

Use Online Resources 72

Think About Your Existing Networks 72

Do Things You Love...72

Volunteer..73

Dealing with Past Failures: Learning from Setbacks.............................73

Workbook Activity: Dealing With Setbacks During BED Recovery 75

Chapter 6: Emotional Triggers—Tackling Guilt, Shame, and
            Emotional Eating.. 81

Dealing With Guilt and Shame...82

Forgive Yourself...82

Forget About Punishments 83

Analyze What Happened 83

Challenge Your Thoughts 83

Take a Time Out 84

Get Professional Help 84

Strategy #3: Developing Emotional Awareness 85

Evaluating Your Emotional Awareness 85

How to Improve Emotional Awareness 89

Learn to Label Your Emotions 89

Mindfulness 90

Question Your Emotions..90

Using your Journal..90

Practice Active Listening 91

Put Yourself in Another's Shoes 91

Stop Complaining...91

Practicing Self-Compassion...92

The Benefits of Self-Compassion 93

How to Practice Self-Compassion..93

Strategy #4: Cultivating Healthy Coping Strategies 94

The Purpose of Coping Strategies..95

Healthy Coping Strategies to Try 96

Guided Imagery 96

Spend Time Outdoors... 96

Be Creative... 96

Deep Breathing 97

Meditation 97

Exercise 97

Journaling...97

Seek Support...98

Taking a Bath/Shower..98

Workbook Activity: Crafting Your Personalized Healthy Coping

Strategies for Binge Eating... 99

Questions 99

Actionable Steps...102

Chapter 7: Healing Your Relationship with Food— Strategies for

Sustainable Recovery 105

Mindful Eating...106

Benefits of Mindful Eating 107

Provides a Moment of Stillness in Our Busy Lives..............107

Helps Identify When You Are Truly Hungry 107

Enjoy Your Food More 108

Make Better Choices Regarding What You Eat 108

You Stop Eating When Full 108

    Appreciate Food More..108

    Let Go of Shame Associated With Eating 109

    Improves Digestion 109

  How to Practice Mindful Eating...109

    Question Your Senses...109

    Spark Your Curiosity 110

    Evaluate Your Hunger 110

    Eat Slower 110

    Tracking Chart 111

Strategy #5: Nourishing Your Body—Balanced Nutrition, Meal
Planning, Recipes, and Building a Healthy, Structured Eating Pattern.........113

  Balanced Nutrition 113

  Meal Planning 114

  Recipes..116

  Structured Eating 123

  The Benefits of Structured Eating 124

  Tips for Implementing Structured Eating 125

Managing Food Cravings—Coping with Triggers 126

Workbook Activity: Designing a Personalized Meal Plan 129

  Step 1: Assess Your Nutritional Needs 130

  Step 2: Define Your Meal Structure 130

  Step 3: Choose Balanced Food Groups 131

  Step 4: Portion Sizes and Serving Guidelines........................131

  Step 5: Meal Prep and Planning 131

  Step 6: Reflective Questions 132

Chapter 8: Thriving Beyond Binge Eating Disorder............137

Strategy #6: Prioritizing Self-Care..138

  The Four Pillars of Self-Care..138

    Physical Self-Care..138

    Emotional Self-Care...140

    Mental Self-Care..140

    Spiritual Self-Care...141

Strategy #7: Body Acceptance and Self-Love—Embracing Your
Unique Beauty 142
    The Four Aspects of Body Image 143
    How to Change Your Body Image 143
Strategy #8: Practicing Positive Affirmations 145
    Benefits of Positive Affirmations 145
    How to Implement Positive Affirmations Daily 146
Workbook Activity: Creating a Daily Self-Care Routine 148
    Step 1: Reflect on Your Needs and Priorities 149
    Step 2: Identify Self-Care Activities 149
    Step 3: Create a Daily Schedule 150
    Step 4: Reflective Questions 150
    Step 5: Implement and Adjust 154
What happens next? 154

Conclusion 159
References 161

INTRODUCTION

Eating disorders affect a greater part of the global population than we could ever imagine. Global statistics between 2000 and 2018 showed that general eating disorders have more than doubled in that time frame by increasing from 3.4% to 7.8% (Rehman, 2020). However, since then, the global COVID-19 pandemic caused eating disorders to rise by 15% in people under 30 in the United States alone (Taquet et al., 2021). The numbers are truly astonishing, and when you consider that these are only the cases that are diagnosed, you begin to realize how much higher it would be if we considered all those who suffer in silence.

Eating disorders are more prevalent than ever before, and although more women are affected than men, the number is not as small as you think. I, myself, have been through it and was surprised to learn that almost 25% of reported cases of eating disorders come from men (Walen, 2016). Once again, the point to emphasize is that these are statistics based on reported cases. Those with eating disorders know that the numbers are probably significantly higher.

Suffering from any eating disorder is hard, but binge eating disorder (BED) is particularly difficult because there is shame and guilt involved. The self-loathing that occurs in the aftermath of binge eating is a problem in itself. It severely clouds your mind and prevents you from seeing yourself clearly. It is extremely hard to step forward and reveal the problem to anyone, let alone tell your friends and family.

How do you explain why you have an eating disorder? Will people just see it as an excuse for your weight? How do you deal with the silent judgment that you are sure happens when you walk into a room? More importantly, how do you admit that you do not know how to stop? If any of these questions sound familiar, then this workbook is definitely for you. I wrote it with this in mind because I know exactly how trapped and helpless you can feel when it comes to this aspect of your life—I have been there.

First and foremost, I want you to know that having a BED does not make you weak, nor does it mean that there is something wrong with you. BED is a complex mental disorder that involves a deep interplay of emotions, psychological factors, and physical responses to food. The fact that you are trying to find ways to overcome it means that you are stronger than you think!

The effects of BED severely impact one's life both physically and psychologically. The physical aspects revolve around bloating, discomfort, weight gain, and decreased quality of life due to high blood pressure, diabetes, and heart disease. The psychological components include issues with body image, constant social comparisons, social isolation, anxiety, and depression (Sheehan & Herman, 2015).

It is not hard to understand how the times we live in can exacerbate BED as well. Not only did the COVID-19 pandemic put us in a bad space mentally, but the lockdown period worsened eating habits overall. Increased use of social media, not only during the lockdown but in general, has made it harder to maintain a positive self-image because you are constantly bombarded with perfect content online. Even though we know that it is curated content and not real life, we are still made to feel like we need to live up to online expectations.

So, how do you overcome a BED when you try to live up to these expectations? Do you go on a strict diet which then leads to even bigger cravings than before? It's almost as if you were destined to fail from the start, so why bother trying?

Well, that's just it—it's the wrong approach. You can't simply address binge eating by adjusting your diet and exercise. You have to delve into the true cause of your binge eating and not everyone will have the same cause, nor do they have the same lifestyle or same BED. As a result, the same approach will never work for everyone. You need a unique approach for each unique case.

This workbook offers a holistic, compassionate, and personalized approach to healing. My BED was triggered by a painful event in my family. I chose to ignore the connection at the time because food gave me the solace I so desperately needed. However, I now firmly believe that true recovery can only be achieved by addressing both the emotional and physical aspects of the disorder. There is no silver bullet approach that is going to miraculously cure you overnight. You have to work through your eating disorder step by step and be willing to commit to lifelong self-compassion and understanding.

Numerous people have overcome BED and inspired many to do the same, including me. It is only when you address the root cause of your eating disorder that you can begin to move forward and live your life to the fullest. At this moment, your eating disorder is stopping you from reaching your true potential and you need to start working toward a healthier and happier future.

To do this, you need to build a personalized toolkit that will begin your journey of self-discovery, self-compassion, and self-empowerment. This workbook provides eight actionable strategies that will help you do this. It will guide you in identifying and managing your triggers, cultivating a healthy relationship with food, and will place in front of you a roadmap to recovery. There is no shame in admitting you have a BED, and there is definitely no shame in wanting change in your life. It is never too late to work toward a healthier life no matter your circumstance. You are worthy of happiness and of having a life free from the shackles of BED. However, before we begin this journey, I want you to know that it will not be easy. There will be ups and downs as with anything in life. It's important to view setbacks as opportunities for learning and growth instead of failures. You have to be patient and remember that even small steps forward are still progress. Let's take the first step together and get started. You can do this!

CHAPTER 1

UNDERSTANDING BINGE EATING DISORDER—UNVEILING THE BASICS

Eating disorders are serious mental illnesses, not lifestyle choices.

—DEMI LOVATO

Often when people speak about binge eating, our first thoughts go to over-eating while watching movies or hanging out with our friends. In fact, many of us are familiar with that feeling of eating to the point where we begin to feel uncomfortable. However, in these cases, binge eating is not a problem as it is a once-in-a-while occurrence. It may make one feel a little sick or guilty, but it's all done in good fun. It's almost like being a kid again and often, it is done in the company of others. So, if we all do this from time to time, what makes binge eating a disorder? This chapter will help you better understand BED and help you identify the symptoms and effects that it causes.

What Is Binge Eating Disorder?

Binge Eating Disorder (BED) is not simply overeating—this is a common mistake that many people make. It is defined as a mental health disorder that results in people consuming large amounts of food in short periods of time. It differs from the occasional overeating in that it occurs frequently, is often done alone, and is accompanied by intense feelings of shame, guilt, and embarrassment (Turner, 2016). BED affects all age groups, genders, and weights, and is possibly one of the most misunderstood eating disorders despite being one of the most prevalent. This is because people cannot see how this eating order impacts an individual. Whereas anorexia is easily recognizable and bulimia has distinct patterns of eating and purging, BED is more of an invisible eating disorder. Most people binge eat in secret and even though this can lead to weight gain, it is not always the case.

BED is not a result of a person's eating habits. In fact, a person's binge eating is the result of mental health problems. People binge eat to make themselves feel better or to forget what is troubling them. It is often done absentmindedly, without any control or feelings other than relief. However, the relief is short-lived as afterward, negative feelings arise when you realize what you have done. These negative feelings can also fuel a need to binge eat once again to feel better. This produces a cycle that is hard to break, but not impossible. You have to address the root cause of your BED, which can be difficult in itself, but necessary to break free from this disorder.

BED has the potential to be life-threatening if left untreated. Unfortunately, the one thing that I discovered is that it is all too easy for people to dismiss the disorder and just chastise you for eating too much. This is dangerous as it causes you to hide your binging from everyone and sometimes worsens it altogether. BED takes away from your quality of life. It affects your physical and mental health and is often misdiagnosed as it can be present alongside other eating disorders and mental health issues. This almost makes BED a silent killer as it affects far more people than we know.

Journaling

Let's take a brief pause here and discuss the value of maintaining a journal as you progress through this workbook.

A journal isn't just a place to write; for those recovering from BED, it's a therapeutic tool that offers numerous benefits. It aids in cultivating self-awareness, monitoring eating habits, identifying triggers, expressing emotions, tracking progress, and so much more. Simply put, it's your personal companion on the road to BED recovery, fostering insight, strategy, and healing.

As we embark on this recovery journey together, we'll explore these benefits in greater depth.

Before getting too far down the road though, I highly recommend acquiring a quality notebook. This will serve as your dedicated BED recovery journal moving forward.

So, why wait? Start today with your journal by your side, jotting down any thoughts that may arise, regardless of their perceived significance, as you continue progressing through this roadmap to recovery. Furthermore, on this journey, I will occasionally provide additional guidance for you by suggesting supplementary journal entries to enhance your overall experience.

What Causes BED?

BED is caused by a variety of factors. In fact, this eating disorder is still being researched because it is not fully understood. BED can be caused by one or a combination of the following factors:

Perfectionism

We live in a world where we are surrounded by picture-perfect images. Whether it be advertisements or images on social media, the idea of perfectionism runs rife. Perfectionists may be triggered by these images when they begin to believe that they cannot achieve society's idea of what is perfect. This can affect one's mental health and their pursuit of perfectionism can affect their eating habits. In terms of BED, perfectionism can lead to individuals binge eating to achieve a "perfect" weight or out of annoyance that they cannot achieve the perfect body. Your mind tells you *Why bother?* If you can't have the perfect body, what's stopping you from eating? However, when this happens continuously, you risk developing BED.

Dieting

It is not uncommon for those with BED to be serial dieters. Everyone knows how frustrating a diet can be. However, if you limit your calories drastically, there is always a point where the urge to binge takes over. A simple cheat meal can turn into a binge eating session with the promise to yourself that you will continue the diet with more discipline after you binge just one more time. This can become a dangerous cycle, especially if you begin to gain weight instead of losing it when dieting. You will then push yourself harder to diet, resulting in larger cravings or urges to binge.

Mood Disorders

A shocking statistic surrounding BED is that 80% of people with BED also have another mood disorder (Mandl, 2019). This can include Post-Traumatic Stress Disorder (PTSD), bipolar disorder, depression, or anxiety. The relationship between these disorders and BED is bidirectional. This means that mood disorders can trigger BED and BED can trigger the existing mood disorder.

Trauma

Many people have their BED triggered by traumatic life experiences. Whether it was in their childhood or later in life, trauma can have a strong hold on their actions, thoughts, and behaviors. My BED was caused by a traumatic experience in my family life and it was not until I worked through my trauma that I was able to recover. However, many people don't see how the two are correlated. Their binge eating is triggered unconsciously when past traumas are remembered. In fact, it is not uncommon that people won't even know they have binged until they are done eating. Just as they try to block out their trauma, they will block out their binge eating as well.

Bullying

The school bully has never been quite as dangerous as they are now. Not only has bullying at schools escalated, but the internet has given bullies a place to hide. Cyberbullying among children and adults is on the rise, and when this bullying targets one's weight or physical appearance, the effects can be terrifying. BED is just one of the issues that may arise as a result of bullying. People may eat as a way to comfort themselves after personal attacks, as a way to forget, or as an act of defeat. It all depends on their state of mind at that point in time and the specifics of the bullying they face.

Drug and Alcohol Use

The link between drug and alcohol abuse and BED is not fully understood. What is known is that the driving reasons behind people's choice to abuse substances are usually the same reasons they binge eat. Therefore, drug and alcohol abuse may not necessarily cause BED, but there is a higher chance that one may lead to the other. Furthermore, those trying to recover from substance abuse may turn to food which can lead to BED. The opposite is also true in many instances (The Recovery Village, 2021).

Genetics

There is a larger chance of family members having BED due to genetics (Bakalar et al., 2015). Not only does BED become normalized behavior when exposed to binge eating from a young age, but the genes carried by family members can also make one more susceptible to binge eating. Certain genes make one more sensitive to dopamine, which is a neurotransmitter in the brain associated with rewards. Thus, the good feeling one has when eating is more intense, making bingeing more attractive.

Obesity

People with obesity also have a higher risk of BED. It could be the reason behind their weight gain, or it may have developed after. Feelings of helplessness, shame, and guilt all lead to binge eating to feel better. Unfortunately, this can have serious health impacts and can even lead to early death.

The above causes of BED are by no means an extensive list. Researchers are still looking into this eating disorder and learning more every day. BED is not exactly shrouded in mystery, but the fact that most cases are hidden or also include other psychological disorders makes it more difficult to identify and diagnose. It becomes a chicken and egg situation that often leaves people with BED confused if it is not fully explained. At the end of the day, you have to be able to identify the symptoms and signs of BED before you begin working on identifying your triggers.

Identifying Symptoms and Signs

Identifying the symptoms of BED is easier if you are trying to evaluate your eating habits as compared to trying to identify the symptoms in someone else. This is because people suffering from BED are experts at hiding their bingeing. Talking from experience, I used to ensure that I had time away from people so that I could binge without anyone seeing. It was not necessarily something I looked forward to, but something that I knew I had to do to hide my eating habits from others. This was before I was diagnosed with BED—I just didn't want to be judged by others. Besides hiding your eating from others, here are some other symptoms and signs of a BED.

Stashing Food Away/Missing Food

Hoarding food to fuel your binge eating in private is one of the signs of BED. It is one thing to have a stash of candy that you hide away from your kids or siblings, but having a large amount of food hidden away in random places is not the same. People with roommates or partners with BED may realize that there is food missing from the fridge or pantry on a regular basis. One thing that also surprises everyone is that binge eating does not only involve junk food—healthy foods count as well. Thus, even hiding healthy foods in unhealthy amounts for a binge session is considered hoarding food to feed your binge eating habits.

Social Isolation

People with BED tend to isolate themselves in order to hide their eating. This results in them canceling on friends and staying at home more and more frequently. It is a common symptom that is also related to depression. Usual activities and interacting with others no longer bring you joy because you feel uncomfortable. It may be because you are avoiding eating in public, discussing your weight, or simply because you don't want to be confronted with food in a public setting. You feel more comfortable not just eating, but being on your own in general.

Finding Empty Food Packaging

A friend of mine used to wake up in the morning only to discover her bed and floor littered with empty food packaging. They had been binge eating at night without even registering it. This is a common occurrence among those with BED. You will only register how much you ate after finding the empty food packaging that surrounds you. It could be in your home, your car, or even in your office. You may also find the need to hide the packaging from others. People who live with individuals with BED often discover their eating habits when discovering empty food packaging hidden in the trash.

Loss of Control

One of the most common symptoms of BED is the loss of control one feels when eating. It's as if you are not in charge of your body during the time that you are eating. You cannot stop yourself from eating and you don't have any thoughts or feelings while eating. It can also feel that there is no way to overcome BED because you have no control over your actions.

Feelings of Shame, Disgust, and Guilt After Eating

After a binge eating session, people with BED often experience intense feelings of disgust, shame, and guilt. This is directed at themselves and their eating. BED can be accompanied by low self-esteem or a negative self-image that intensifies with these feelings after binge eating. There is also intense disappointment at not being able to control oneself when eating.

Eating Not Triggered by Hunger

Most people eat when they are hungry and stop when they are full, but when it comes to people with BED, eating is neither triggered by hunger nor stopped by feeling satiated. This is why it feels like there is no control when it comes to BED and why it is so harmful to your health. Eating continues well past the feeling of being full and you will feel uncomfortable or sick by the end of a binge eating session. People with BED are not eating large amounts because they are hungry. They don't have large appetites and they definitely cannot just stop eating because they should.

Eating Rapidly

Another symptom of BED is that binge eating sessions are not long. People eat a large amount of food in a short amount of time. That is one of the diagnostic criteria of BED. Those with a BED tend to eat an amount of food that is larger than "normal" for one person in a two-hour time period. I emphasized normal in the above sentence because everyone has a different definition of a normal amount of food due to different appetites—but that's a whole different story. The point is, BED results in people eating quickly and often without any sort of inhibition, which is why they feel uncomfortable and sick afterward.

Gastrointestinal Issues

The last symptom that I want to go through is gastrointestinal issues. These issues are both a sign and an effect of BED. Due to the rapid eating of large volumes of food, gastrointestinal issues such as acid reflux, indigestion, constipation, and diarrhea may occur. It also depends on the type of foods that are consumed during a binge eating session and a person's current digestive health. However, despite these issues, sufferers of BED will not stop eating even though they know it would be best for their health.

These are the symptoms that will help you identify a BED. You will notice that I did not put weight gain on this list. The reason for this is that although there is a link between BED and obesity, weight gain is not necessarily a symptom of the disorder. People may or may not gain weight depending on their lifestyle and unique bodies. Some may have a fast metabolism, while others may diet or exercise to hide their BED. Therefore, weight gain cannot be a reliable sign or symptom of BED like those listed above.

Recognizing the Effects of BED

The effects of BED can vary greatly. Each person is different and how their BED affects them can be completely different to how it affects another person. Furthermore, the effects can be physical, mental, emotional, psychological, or even financial in extreme cases. It can also be divided into short-term and long-term effects. Let's take a closer look.

Short-Term Effects

The short-term effects of BED are those which show up soon after the onset of the disorder. They are quick changes and often, treatment for the disorder at this stage is easier than it would be later on.

Digestive Issues

The first and most prominent short-term effect of BED is digestive issues. Even though bodies vary, our stomachs can only stretch to accommodate a certain amount of food and liquid. Once we surpass this amount, we begin to feel uncomfortable or possibly nauseated (Balzora, 2022). The type of food that is eaten can also cause problems in your gut such as constipation or diarrhea.

The real danger of BED is that you don't register these issues until you are done eating. It is possible to continue eating after you are physically full. These digestive issues are considered a short-term effect because, over time, it is possible for your body to become accustomed to eating such large amounts in short periods of time. This does not mean that these issues will disappear completely, but rather that it will take larger amounts of food to trigger them.

Weight Gain

As mentioned earlier, not all people with a BED exhibit weight gain. However, fluctuations in weight can be a common short-term effect in some individuals. This is especially true if they are binge eating and not very active in their daily lives. Many people with BED do not see a need to do anything to counteract their binges, and therefore may experience weight gain. However, they may also try to hide it from others, which is why people with BED tend to avoid social situations.

Trouble Sleeping

People with BED have trouble sleeping which stems from two main causes. The first is that binge eating will prevent them from sleeping due to digestive upset. Although eating a large meal can make most people feel sleepy, people with BED may have difficulty sleeping due to the uncomfortableness they experience. The second reason is due to the mental upset that accompanies BED. People may feel anxious or angry or even be saddened by their eating habits and that can prevent them from gaining any form of mental or physical rest.

Long-Term Effects

The long-term effects of BED are much more severe. In many cases, BED can go on for years before a professional diagnosis is made or before anyone, including the patient, discovers that there is an eating disorder to address. Dealing with the long-term effects is not impossible, but they do require more intense interventions and, unfortunately, some damage cannot be undone. However, they can be managed to give people a better quality of life and relief from their BED.

Obesity

People with a BED have a higher chance of being obese. This is due to the nature of the disorder as people eat more food than necessary and do not feel the need to do anything about it. If a BED goes undiagnosed or ignored for a long period, obesity slowly creeps in as people gain more and more weight.

Furthermore, because it happens over time, people judge BED sufferers as just being overweight and lazy. This is truly unfortunate as people with BED already have a negative self-image and low self-esteem. Judging them harshly about their weight can worsen their condition and put their health, and life, at risk.

Heart Disease

As a result of unhealthy eating habits and weight gain, high cholesterol levels and blood pressure can eventually put a strain on an individual's heart. Heart disease is a common long-term effect that occurs in people with BED. Along with the strain caused by eating, there are also high levels of stress and anxiety that a person has to deal with when suffering from BED. This leads to a continued high level of cortisol in the blood which can cause problems with blood pressure and heart failure (Yamaji et al., 2009).

Diabetes

Type 2 diabetes is another long-term consequence of BED. This happens as a result of poor eating habits, insulin resistance, and lack of physical activity. Often, type 2 diabetes can lead to more severe health risks like heart, kidney, and eye disease, along with increasing chances of a stroke and nerve damage. These implications can severely hinder a person's life by limiting vision and movement.

Isolation

Social isolation is indeed a long-term effect of BED. As much as it begins early on in the disorder, it can escalate to a point where a person no longer interacts with others. Weddings, parties, and even work events may be avoided in an attempt to hide their binge eating or avoid being judged by others.

This can hinder an individual's chances of progressing in their career, meeting a potential life partner, or even making new friends. As such, people with BED miss out on reaching their true potential if they allow the disorder to continue.

These effects exclude the toll BED takes on a person's mental health, the financial strain it can put people under, and the impact it has on families. BED is a lot more serious than many people think. This is partially because of the name and also because of the lack of knowledge surrounding the disorder. Binge eating is not the same as binge-watching television series. It has far more serious consequences and in the next chapter, I hope that you will begin to see why we need to address any form of BED sooner rather than later.

CHAPTER 2

THE PREVALENCE OF BINGE EATING DISORDER—KNOWING YOU'RE NOT ALONE

Binge on life. Purge negativity. Starve guilty feelings.

—ANONYMOUS

Having a BED is anything but easy. People scoff at it because they believe you just need to control your greed or obsession with food—but it's not that simple. Furthermore, because society is so quick to judge, many people with a BED feel ashamed to admit they have a problem. I clearly remember how long I lived with my secret shame and guilt. I was too embarrassed to speak to anyone because I didn't want to be judged. It was clear what others would think of my weight and my eating—it was better to suffer in silence, on my own.

However, what I didn't know at the time is that BED is more prevalent than I could have ever imagined. Through my recovery, I met more and more people who felt exactly like I did—alone, ashamed, and hesitant to seek help. This is why I wanted to go through the prevalence of BED in this chapter. I want you to know that you are not alone in this battle and speaking up is not admitting to your shame, it's the beginning of letting it go.

Statistics and Data on BED

Before we jump into the current statistics and data surrounding BED, it is important to note that these statistics are based on reported cases. I've mentioned it before, and I'm sure you understand, the numbers are probably significantly higher. Many people don't step forward to get help. In fact, even among those who do come forward, 60% of them are still not sure whether they need treatment (Linardon et al., 2020).

Couple this with the fact that a BED will, on average, only be diagnosed three years after onset (Gill & Kaplan, 2020) and you can already begin to see the true danger that a BED presents. Let's take a closer look at the other facts and figures behind this disorder.

Prevalence in Adults

When we talk about the prevalence of a disorder, we talk about how common it is. In the case of BED, the prevalence is much higher than that of other eating disorders. The prevalence of BED in adults is estimated to be 1.2%, which is four times and twice as much as the prevalence of bulimia and anorexia, respectively (National Institute of Mental Health, 2017).

In addition, the lifetime prevalence (how common it is for an adult to experience BED in their life) is 2.3% (Erskine & Whiteford, 2018), with women being twice as likely to experience BED than men. Another interesting fact is that although it is possible for children to have BED, the average onset of the disorder is approximately 25 years (Hudson et al., 2007). This is much later than the onset of other eating disorders.

From these prevalence statistics, we can tell that BED is a much bigger problem than other eating disorders even though less is known about it. These numbers will likely increase as diagnostics improve and doctors learn more about separating BED from other disorders.

Prevalence in Children and Teenagers

Are you ready for another shocking statistic? According to new research by López-Gil et al. (2023), 22% of children exhibit some form of disordered eating. Globally, the prevalence of BED among children is 0.7% (Rozzell et al., 2019) and in the United States alone BED has a prevalence of 1.1% among children between 10 and 11 years of age (Murray et al., 2022). Eating disorders are, therefore, not just a problem in teenagers and adults, children as young as 9 have been diagnosed with a BED.

Furthermore, there is no difference between genders at this stage, with differences only occurring later in adolescence (Rozzell et al., 2019). In fact, when considering research done internationally, twice as many female adolescents (26% vs. 13%) have had an incidence of binge eating at least once (Marzilli et al., 2018). What is truly worrying is that this age group is at an impressionable age. Showing any signs of BED, whether diagnosed or not, can lead to lower self-esteem, body dissatisfaction, and depression.

However, despite these statistics, methods for evaluating BED in children and adolescents are a bit difficult. Diagnosing binge eating in this age group poses a challenge for healthcare providers because the substantial food intake in children can be attributed to their active lifestyle and the natural growth processes, especially during growth spurts and puberty.

Since BED is essentially seen as eating more than one person requires in a short time, simply evaluating caloric intake is not reliable. Anyone who has witnessed an active teenage boy eating during a growth spurt can understand why this would be difficult to identify in youngsters.

Therefore, medical professionals tend to interview children or observe their eating to determine if there is any loss of control when eating (Bohon, 2019). Having a BED early in life also puts children at risk of obesity, mental health issues, and abnormal cardiac function as they get older. Thus, early diagnosis is vital.

Health Effects

We've discussed the effects of BED previously, but putting some numbers to them helps to put things in perspective. A recent US-based study was instrumental in gathering the risk factors associated with BED. The results showed that 94% of people with BED reported comorbid mental health problems and almost 23% attempted suicide.

Of the people with BED and comorbidity with mental health issues the study reported, 70% were mood disorders, 68% were substance use disorders, 59% were anxiety disorders, 49% were borderline personality disorder, and 32% were post-traumatic stress disorder (Keski-Rahkonen, 2021).

Furthermore, almost 40% of people who suffer from BED are obese (Heal & Smith, 2021), 15% are considered morbidly obese (Hudson et al., 2007), and 20% suffer from excessive alcohol use (Bogusz et al., 2020).

These figures begin to paint a clearer picture of what BED is truly capable of. Even though it was identified in 1959, it was not until 2013 that it was formally recognized as a disorder on its own (Schaeffer, 2015). This is why research is still ongoing to discover the true extent of its effects and more about how to treat the disorder.

Treatment Statistics

The good news about treatment that everyone needs to know is that, on average, between 84 and 97% of people who seek treatment for BED report an improvement in their health. Treatment options for BED include therapy and medication, with both providing similar results (Gill & Kaplan, 2020).

In addition, at least 35% of people who try self-help methods based on Cognitive Behavioral Theory (CBT) have recovered fully from BED (Linardon, 2018). Thus, one should never feel like there is no chance of recovery if they cannot afford CBT sessions with a therapist. Seeking help does not come with a price tag, it comes with the reward of recovery.

Common Misconceptions and Stigmas Surrounding BED

Now that we have been through the facts surrounding BED, it's time to look at some of the myths. People are quick to brush BED aside because of these misconceptions—even those who have the disorder use these as reasons not to seek help. So, let's take a look at how ignorance can lead society astray.

BED Is Only a Problem in Overweight/Obese People

This is one of the biggest misconceptions surrounding BEDs and one of the main reasons that people will not recognize a BED in those closest to them. People of all weights can have a BED and although they may not purge, they may intensively diet trying to stop any weight gain.

Furthermore, everyone's digestive system and gut microbiome are different and react differently to eating large amounts of food. A BED does not have "a body type" and the sooner we accept this, the sooner we get rid of the stigma surrounding BED.

Children Can't Have BED

As discussed earlier, children as young as 9 can have a BED. Yes, it is harder to identify, but medical professionals have been able to assess both eating habits and the psychology behind children's binge eating. Furthermore, since BED has a strong genetic link, people who have BED are likely to have kids who develop or are at higher risk of developing a BED. Thus, it is important to not simply dismiss a child's eating habits without evaluation, especially if there has been previous trauma or exposure to someone with an eating disorder.

Going on a Diet Will Cure BED

If binge eating is a problem, people should just stop eating so much and go on a diet, right? Wrong! BED cannot be cured by simply going on a diet. In fact, dieting is one of the major contributors to BEDs in the first place. Therefore, going on a diet can actually worsen a person's BED. The root cause of the disorder has to be addressed for a person to have a healthy relationship with food. There is no other way around it.

Overeating and Binge Eating Are the Same

Overeating is definitely not the same as binge eating. To overeat is a choice—most people have experienced overeating during Thanksgiving, Christmas, or even the neighborhood barbecue. People who have BED do not have a choice—they have no control over their binge eating.

Furthermore, the time taken to eat a large amount of food is far less in BED than in overeating. Overeating tends to be a leisurely event, people are usually in the company of others and enjoying their food as they eat. On the other hand, those with BED will binge eat alone and tend not to even taste or register what they are eating.

Men Don't Get BED

There is a lot of stigma surrounding men and eating disorders in general, it's not just with BED. However, I can tell you from experience that men can definitely get BED. The problem with this misconception is that it makes men seem weak for having an eating disorder and causes many men to suffer in silence. I was one of them, I know what it feels like to hide because I didn't want people to think I'm weak. I now know just how prevalent eating disorders are in men and it was shocking, even for me, to wrap my head around the fact that BED can affect anyone and everyone.

There Are No Long-Term Effects of BED

Another large misconception I wanted to cover is that people don't believe that there are long-term effects of BED. It ties in with the misconceptions that only overweight people binge eat and a diet is the answer to BED. You see, people think that the only effect of binge eating is weight gain—and once you lose the weight, the problem will disappear. The truth is that there are definitely long-term effects of BED. Even though people may recover from BED, they may still suffer the effects of the disorder long after. These effects include both physical and mental effects that could impact a person's life permanently.

These misconceptions are all a matter of ignorance. Many people lack knowledge about BED and draw their own conclusions, which, in turn, fuels the stigma surrounding the disorder. As a result, people are scared to even contemplate seeking help or getting a proper diagnosis because they know exactly what others will say when they find out. This is why it is so important to challenge the stigma surrounding eating disorders. You don't have to go out there and debate with everyone—but now that you know better, spread the knowledge so others can, too.

Understanding Co-Occurring Disorders

A co-occurring disorder refers to a mental disorder that accompanies another one. In the case of BED, research has shown that almost 79% of people with BED have at least one co-occurring disorder.

Some examples of co-occurring disorders are:

- **Mood Disorders:** It is not uncommon for those with BED to also have a co-occurring mood disorder such as depression or bipolar disorder.
- **Anxiety Disorder:** The anxiety associated with anticipating your next binge, if someone will find out, or with the aftermath of a binge can all lead to an anxiety disorder. However, it is also possible that the anxiety disorder was already present and BED developed as a coping mechanism.
- **Post-Traumatic Stress Disorder (PTSD):** PTSD is a common cause of eating disorders. It is usually present before the onset of BED.

- **Obsessive-Compulsive Disorder (OCD):** Obsessive-Compulsive Disorder is commonly found in those with BED. It stems from perfectionism and obsessive beliefs surrounding one's self-image.

- **Borderline Personality Disorder:** This co-occurring disorder is one that severely impacts a person's ability to regulate their emotions, causing extreme mood swings and erratic behaviors.

- **Trichotillomania:** This is a disorder that causes an individual to pull out their hair. It can range in severity and is a form of OCD.

- **Substance Abuse/Alcoholism:** Many people turn to substance abuse to deal with their BED. It is an unsurprisingly common co-occurring disorder as it is a similar coping mechanism to BED.

- **Self-Harm:** This is a dangerous co-occurring disorder. People with BED may self-harm as a way to punish themselves for binge eating. In fact, some may even use binge eating as a way to self-harm.

Workbook Activity: Reflection on Personal Experiences and Insights

Now that we have covered what BED is, what the symptoms and effects are, and the facts and misconceptions surrounding the disorder, it is time for you to reflect on your personal experiences and insights relating to BED. The following exercise will help you truly gain insight into your thoughts and help you identify patterns that you may not have been aware of previously. To complete this exercise, use the space provided below to fill in your answers. If you don't want to write in the workbook, then grab a separate notebook or open up a blank document on your laptop. Remember, it is not easy to reflect on painful experiences, but the only way this exercise will work is if you answer the questions honestly and thoughtfully. Let's get started.

Reflective Questions

1. When did you first notice patterns of binge eating in your life? Think back to the earliest memories you have of binge eating.

_____

_____

_____

_____

2. Identify specific triggers or events that led to a binge eating episode in your life.

_____

_____

_____

_____

3. Are there any specific thoughts or beliefs that lead you to binge eat?

_____

_____

_____

_____

4. Think about how you feel before, during, and after a binge-eating episode. Is there a definitive pattern to your emotions?

_____

_____

_____

_____

5. Has binge eating affected your physical and emotional health over time? Think back to before your binge eating began to help you identify specific differences.

_____

_____

_____

_____

6. Consider your personal and professional relationships. How has your BED affected these relationships?

_____

_____

_____

_____

7. How has BED affected your relationship with yourself? How do you see yourself?

_____

_____

_____

_____

8. Have you tried to manage your binge eating in the past? What strategies or coping mechanisms do you use? Divide them into two lists: those which help and those which don't.

_____

_____

_____

_____

9. Can you think of any events, situations, or people that have made it challenging or impossible for you to overcome BED?

_____

_____

_____

_____

10. If you consider the course of your binge eating over time, can you identify any fluctuations in your binge eating? Dig deeper to try and find out what may have caused these fluctuations.

_____

_____

_____

_____

11. Have you had any breakthrough moments during your BED? What happened leading up to these moments?

_____

_____

_____

_____

12. What lessons have you learned about yourself and your relationship with food thus far?

_____

_____

_____

_____

Remember to be honest when answering these questions. Just as it is hurtful to be judged by others, you should never be judgmental of yourself. Be kind to yourself as you openly reflect on your experiences, thoughts, and behaviors. You should also take your time and remember that there is no rush to the finish line. Self-reflection is not easy and delving deep into your emotions and thoughts will take time.

Be as specific as you can with your answers and write down examples so that it is easier to come back to and remember throughout your journey to recovery. You can add to your answers at any point if you remember something after answering them the first time. You can also share your reflections with a therapist or support group to help gain further insight into yourself, your BED, and your road to recovery.

This exercise is crucial to begin your journey to recovery. Before we begin introducing the strategies that you can use to overcome BED, we just have to work through one more thing—identifying the nature of your BED cycle.

CHAPTER 3

THE BED CYCLE—UNDERSTANDING THE VICIOUS CYCLE OF BINGE EATING

Don't let your mind bully your body.

—JUNE TOMASO-WOOD

BED is very much a vicious cycle that people struggle with. People have different triggers that bring on a binge eating episode, and the binge eating episode may fuel emotions that trigger them once more. The added burden of comorbidities often makes breaking this cycle extremely difficult because one disorder feeds the other. Working through the exercise in the previous chapter may have helped you identify your BED cycle, but this chapter will give you a clearer perspective if things are still hazy.

Restrictive Diets

One of the most common BED cycles revolves around restrictive eating. We live in a world where the idea of the perfect body is thrown in our faces whether we want to see it or not. Every social media platform, advertisement on television, and billboard we see shows us images of perfection. Society is made to believe that we should look a certain way and be a certain weight, and that we shouldn't be happy until we attain this perfection.

Many of us even know that this perfection is unattainable because it's not real, but still we crave it because the seed has already been planted. This is arguably one of the reasons why most people are unhappy—they cannot achieve this level of perfection. The constant comparison of bodies, careers, relationships, and lifestyles makes everyone miserable; blind to the consumerism that feeds these perfect images and curated content.

So, what do we do? We begin to hate the way we look, despise our jobs for not making us millionaires, and chastise our partners for not doing more. The constant search for something better leaves us empty and when we try to attain the perfect bodies, we end up doing more harm than good. We begin to restrict ourselves because we believe that it's the best way to get what we want. There are countless diet programs available that all claim that they will give you the body that you want—you just have to cut out carbohydrates, sugars, meat, or solid foods. However, have you noticed that in restricting yourself from these foods, your body begins to crave them even more? How many of us fail our diets because we decide to cheat and tell ourselves that we'll make up for it the next day by restricting ourselves even more?

Our bodies are not meant to be restricted from eating. From a survival perspective, our bodies require food to function. If you take away food, our instincts kick in and we try to find the food we require to survive. As much as diets still provide us with sustenance, our bodies do not register it because they know that it is less than we are accustomed to.

ALLEN CROSS

Thus, our brains become hyper-focused on what we are missing out on and constantly send signals that tell us that we need to eat the one thing we're trying to avoid. This is why when you cut out carbs from your diet, you are constantly craving carbs. It's not withdrawal symptoms as is the case with addiction, it's a survival instinct because our bodies should not be deprived of whole food groups.

Therefore, it is a common occurrence for those who frequently diet to inadvertently pick up more weight. The restrictive nature of fad diets increases the chances of a binge eating episode. In turn, binge eating results in feelings of disappointment, guilt, and shame for failing the diet, which in turn causes people to restrict their eating even more. Thus begins a cycle of dieting and binge eating that can easily lead to BED. This is why "yo-yo" dieting is dangerous and unhealthy. You are not addressing your relationship with food and instead building bad habits that make a BED cycle possible.

The Pressure to Eat: Emotional and External Factors

Emotional eating is something every one of us has experienced at some point in our lives whether we were aware of it or not. Food is so deeply intertwined in our lives that it is a part of our good times and our bad times. Who hasn't overeaten during Thanksgiving dinner? When there's a death in the family, people bring food over to the house as a form of comfort, and when your kid does something good, don't you reward them with ice cream? Food becomes associated with our emotions whether we like it or not. This is why we have our favorite comfort foods when the weather is bad and we have cake when we celebrate a birthday.

The more you delve into your past, the more you will realize the connections food has to our lives and emotions. Nevertheless, emotional eating is not the same as binge eating. As much as you eat to feel better or numb your emotions, there is no loss of control when eating.

However, if your emotions go into overdrive after eating, with feelings of shame and guilt arising, there is a strong chance that your emotional eating has the potential to turn into BED over time. This is because you may feel the need to binge eat to make you feel better and drown out the shame and guilt—and when you realize what you have done, you begin a BED cycle.

Our emotions are also tied to disorders such as depression, anxiety, and stress. When these disorders become chronic conditions, it is easy for food and binge eating to become a coping mechanism to deal with them. Furthermore, the relationship between the disorders is bidirectional, meaning one affects the other. Thus, it creates another form of BED cycle with each disorder feeding the other.

For example, people who suffer from chronic stress may binge eat as a way to feel less stressed or cope with what is happening. The underlying reason is actually the high cortisol levels released during times of stress which consequently increase hunger. Your body reacts in this way because it is trying to gain fuel or energy to deal with what is causing you stress. However, in the case of binge eating, you are not satisfying this hunger, but eating to relieve the stress you feel. Once you realize the amount of food you have eaten, your stress levels may rise again; thereby restarting the cycle.

External environmental factors that influence binge eating refer to what an individual is exposed to daily. A person who has low self-esteem and suffers from a negative self-image may be easily swayed by peer pressure, bullying, and social media. They may feel self-conscious or embarrassed depending on what they are exposed to. As such, they start dieting or restricting their eating, which in turn

ALLEN CROSS

leads to binge eating when they cannot maintain a strict diet. Then they are once again faced with negative emotions that feed a BED cycle.

Another common environmental factor is entangled with the biological factor of genetics. If a person is exposed to family members who binge eat, they are more likely to develop BED themselves. Although genetics play a role, the fact that they could be exposed to binge eating from a young age means that there is also an environmental factor as well. It contributes to your relationship with food and you see it as normal because everyone in your home also eats the same. Thus, you resist change because you feel like people are asking you to change who you are or to go against your family. This could trigger a BED cycle and keep you stuck in believing that you are right and the world is against you.

The Aftermath: Shame and Self-Blame

One of the crucial points of a BED cycle is the shame and self-blame that follows a binge eating episode. It's not a simple matter of "*Oh, I really shouldn't have eaten that,*" but rather an intense feeling of guilt because it was the wrong thing to do. The shame and self-blame worsen the negativity associated with a binge by telling you that there is something wrong with you. The problem with this is that all these feelings stem from untruths. There is nothing wrong with you and eating is not wrong.

It is your relationship with food and your views about food that need to be addressed. We are constantly told which foods are good or bad for us, and we automatically feel guilty for consuming anything considered bad. This negative thought pattern is amplified when it comes to binge eating due to the amount of "bad" foods that are consumed. Subsequently, you are faced with two options: you can start restricting yourself and try to stop your bingeing, or you can binge more to escape what you are feeling. Both of which contribute to strengthening the binge eating cycle.

This is why it is so important to recognize these negative thought patterns and how they contribute to a BED cycle. In most cases, our thoughts and emotions fuel these cycles, and it is not until we deal with them that we can move forward with our recovery.

The previous exercise helped you identify your personal experiences and insights regarding BED. It may have given you an idea of the patterns associated with your binge eating but the next activity will help you map your BED cycle in its entirety.

Workbook Activity: Mapping Your BED Cycle

Identifying your BED cycle gives you a clear idea of the sequence of events that lead to your binge eating. It includes environmental and emotional triggers, memories, past events, and negative thought patterns that go unnoticed until you start paying attention. It can be a somewhat painful or difficult experience, especially if you are trying to forget past traumas. However, in bringing awareness to your BED cycle, you empower yourself by getting the right information to develop effective strategies to work through your BED. It will allow you to break the cycle and make positive, sustainable changes that will change your life for the better.

So, take a deep breath and grab a pen and notebook or write directly in the space provided below as we work through the steps of mapping your BED cycle.

Step 1

Think of your most recent binge episode. When and where was it? Were you with anyone? Do you recall any specific topics of conversation that may have relevance?

List any and all other details that you can remember. This will be the starting point you need to focus on to map your BED cycle. It is easier to focus on the most recent binge as it will still be fresh in your mind and will be easier to recall certain details.

_____

_____

_____

Step 2 - Stages of your BED

Having identified your latest binge, think about each stage - the moments leading up to the binge, what happened during the binge, and what happened after. Identify and label each stage accordingly. Try to remember as much detail as possible without analyzing too much.

_____

_____

_____

Step 3 - Triggers & Emotions

Think back on each stage of your BED cycle. You have all the details that occurred, so now it is time to start reflecting on the triggers and emotions you experienced. Consider the events, thoughts, or situations that led to each stage. Were there specific triggers and emotions that arose during each stage? Take your time and really delve deep to identify both your triggers and emotions. Remember, you have to be honest with yourself. No one is going to judge you based on your answers—nor should you judge yourself. You can't avoid your feelings forever.

_____

_____

_____

Step 4 - Thoughts & Behaviors

The next step is to identify the thoughts and behaviors you exhibit at each stage of your BED cycle. Go slow at this stage because you don't want to trigger a new binge episode in the process. What were the negative or self-critical thoughts you experienced? What thoughts brought about guilt or shame? Did you have any specific thoughts and/or behaviors while actively bingeing? The more you can identify at each stage of the cycle, the better your chances are of finding a way to break it. Remind yourself of this should things get difficult.

_____

_____

_____

Step 5

Now that you have all the information written down, analyze each stage carefully. Are there any connections or patterns that you can identify? Are there recurring **triggers** or emotions that consistently precede the binge? Do certain **thoughts** or **behaviors** contribute to perpetuating the cycle?

_____

_____

_____

Step 6

The final step involves you answering a few simple reflective questions now that you have all the details laid out in front of you. By answering these questions, you will begin to further understand your BED cycle and all that it entails.

- What common triggers lead to your binge episodes?

_____

_____

- Do your emotions fluctuate throughout the different stages of the cycle? How so?

_____

_____

- What are the negative thoughts or beliefs that arise at each stage of a binge episode?

_____

_____

- Have you identified any particular actions or behaviors that you engage in during the cycle? What are they?

_____

_____

- Did you find any patterns or links between your thoughts, emotions, and behaviors?

_____

_____

- Did you identify any environmental factors or external cues that trigger your binge eating?

_____

_____

- Have you thought about how your BED cycle has impacted your overall health and well-being? How has it physically and emotionally impacted your life?

_____

_____

- What does the aftermath of your binge-eating episode look like?

_____

_____

- Do you have people around you or do you have access to relevant resources during moments that you find challenging or difficult?

_____

_____

- How did this activity of mapping your BED cycle make you feel? What insights or realizations have you discovered?

_____

_____

I know how difficult this exercise can be. It forces you to face emotions and events that you would rather forget. However, I can assure you that this is a crucial step to your recovery and strengthening your relationship with yourself. When you gain a deep understanding of your emotions, thoughts, and actions, you'll become an unstoppable force. Achieving your true potential is only steps away and in the next chapter, we begin looking at the strategies that you can implement to free yourself from BED.

CHAPTER 4

INTRODUCTION TO BED RECOVERY

There is no magic cure, no making it all go away forever.
There are only small steps upward; an easier day, an
unexpected laugh, a mirror that doesn't matter anymore.

— LAURIE HALSE ANDERSON

t's time for us to buckle down and start working toward your recovery from BED. The previous chapters have provided you with valuable information that proves that you are not as alone as you think in this battle. The previous activities have also, no doubt, been enlightening in discovering the extent of your BED cycle and how your emotions, thoughts, and behaviors are affected. Now we begin the road to recovery. In this chapter, and the ones that follow, we will discuss the strategies that will help you with your recovery. You have to begin with the right intentions, the right mindset, and the right expectations—which is what we will be talking about next.

Can BED be Cured?

The all-important question: Can your BED be cured? Treatment of BED and the recovery process is not as simple as swallowing a pill. BED is a complicated disorder that is usually present alongside other comorbidities, which means that more than one issue needs to be addressed. Furthermore, the physical and mental aspects of BED must be treated to ensure true recovery. Otherwise, you would simply be addressing the symptoms and not the cause of the disorder. However, as stated earlier, the statistics for recovery are extremely positive, with 84-97% of people reporting a full recovery (Gill & Kaplan, 2020). For this to be true for you as well, you have to ensure that you get the treatment you need.

Remember, no silver bullet will cure BED overnight and no treatment plan will be exactly the same for everyone. Each case of BED is unique and there is no "one size fits all" treatment option. Depending on the causes of your BED and any existing comorbidities, various combinations of therapy, medication, and self-care may be needed. With this in mind, you can start planning your recovery knowing that it is indeed possible to overcome BED with the correct approach.

The Role of Professional Treatment

Speaking to a professional to begin your recovery process is a must. I know that many people try to begin this journey without any help because they believe it is their burden to bear or that speaking to someone means admitting that you have a problem. There are also the costs involved which you might be hesitant about. However, professional treatment has a definite role in your road to recovery and some resources and clinics are available to you at a minimal cost. A diagnosis by a professional will help you determine which path you need to take in terms of treatment.

Treatment options for BED are dependent on the severity of your disorder, the cause, and any other comorbidities that may or may not have been diagnosed yet. A doctor will be able to evaluate your case by asking several questions related to your binge eating. It is important that you are open and honest with them. You can prepare beforehand so that you are not uncomfortable.

They will ask you many of the questions that were a part of the previous activities, along with others, to help determine any other disorders. It is through these open and honest conversations that you will be able to get the help you need. Treatment options include therapy, medication, and nutrition counseling. You may only need one form of treatment, but in most cases, a combination is often recommended. Let's take a closer look at what each one entails so you have a better idea of what to expect.

Therapy

There is usually some stigma surrounding therapy. People consider it a sign of weakness, or worse yet, make fun of it as being part of a trend. However, there is a reason why talk therapy numbers are rising—not just for mental health issues, but for BED as well. It has nothing to do with newer generations being weaker than previous ones or that people are dealing with more problems now than earlier generations. Instead, as we learn more about ourselves as humans and our mental health, we have begun to understand the importance of seeking help and knowing that it is okay to do so.

People with BED can benefit greatly from therapy and there are different options available that will suit their comfort levels. This makes therapy easier as they can go at their own pace and still achieve positive results with every option. Here are the four main therapy types to consider.

Guided Self-Therapy

This form of therapy is usually the first form that would be recommended by a medical professional. It is when you work through a self-help book, guide, or online resource while also having sessions with a therapist in between. In this way, you work through everything on your own and then still have the benefit of a medical professional guiding you and advising you.

Self-therapy also makes individuals feel like they have more control over their recovery and gives them the privacy to deal with issues on their own. It makes people feel more comfortable as they work through the parts that make them most vulnerable on their own while still having the support of a professional along the way.

Cognitive Behavioral Therapy (CBT)

CBT is based on the fact that our thoughts, feelings, and behaviors are intricately connected. Thus, if we can work on understanding our emotions and reframing our negative thoughts, we can then change our behaviors. For individuals with BED, this form of therapy is highly effective by providing a way to manage BED long-term. If they are successful in reframing negative thoughts, they will be less likely to binge in the future. A therapist usually works through CBT for BED patients in three major phases: the behavioral phase, the cognitive phase, and the maintenance and relapse phase.

The behavioral phase is where one would work with a therapist to identify negative emotions and the behaviors they cause. Essentially, for BED sufferers, this translates to identifying the emotions that cause the different stages of their binge eating cycles.

The cognitive phase is where a therapist will start helping people with BED reframe or restructure their negative thoughts. They work with the patient to help them identify the false and negative thoughts they have and help them restructure these thoughts. In this way, people with BED begin to recognize the negative thought patterns they have developed and the distorted image they have of themselves. This phase is extremely enlightening and helps people connect their thoughts to their behaviors, helping to drive positive change.

The final phase of CBT is the maintenance and relapse prevention stage. This stage is crucial to sustain the progress that one makes during therapy. Effective strategies and contingency plans are developed to help people avoid and deal with possible relapses.

CBT takes time and requires patience. However, with the correct mindset and approach, people can achieve lasting change because they address the cognitive causes of their BED and can develop a more positive self-image.

Dialectical Behavioral Therapy (DBT)

An adaptation of CBT, DBT focuses on how emotions drive our behaviors. Thus, while CBT works with reframing thoughts to discourage negative behaviors, DBT works on building our personal skills so we can regulate our behaviors. There are four main areas within DBT that are addressed for BED treatment. These are mindfulness, emotion regulation, interpersonal effectiveness, and distress tolerance. Working in conjunction with a therapist, people with BED can develop these skills to help them manage and overcome the disorder.

Mindfulness is the practice of being aware of the present moment. When people with BED learn this skill, they can slow down and carefully process what is going on. It prevents ruminating on past occurrences and the anxiety associated with overthinking future outcomes. Mindfulness allows the focus to be on the present moment and the emotions experienced. Thus, a person can carefully process these emotions and ensure that their behaviors are in line with what they want. In this way, negative emotions do not have to fuel binge eating sessions and there is no loss of control as a person remains mindful of their actions.

Emotional regulation is an integral part of DBT treatment for BED. People are taught to identify and control their emotions before they induce unwanted behaviors—in this instance, binge eating. This sounds much easier than it actually is because identifying the emotions that induce binge eating can be difficult. It's not only the negative emotions that can bring on a binge eating episode and until a person identifies what drives their BED cycle, they could be stuck. Emotional regulation is a great skill to build in general because it will help you in everyday situations and drive positive behaviors.

Interpersonal effectiveness refers to skills that help individuals manage their interpersonal relationships more effectively. For people with BED, this means learning how to communicate openly and honestly and being able to communicate their needs in relationships. This helps them build self-confidence, become more assertive, and develop positive personal and professional relationships.

Distress tolerance refers to the development of healthy coping mechanisms that will help people with BED avoid binge eating. In combination with the other components of DBT, they will be able to better recognize the emotions that drive their behaviors and put strategies in place that will help them manage better. In addition, it helps people realize that there will be distressing situations in life that are out of their control, but you can control how you react to them. Therefore, they no longer have to worry about distressing emotions or thoughts leading them off their path to recovery.

Unguided Self-Therapy

Unguided self-therapy refers to a process where an individual opts to proceed with the above methods of therapy without the guidance of a therapist. They use self-help books, guides, workbooks - such as this Roadmap to Recovery we are now working through, or online guides and proceed on their own. Some people prefer to work on their own, and there is nothing wrong with that. However, it can be more challenging because there is no one to hold you accountable. You might find yourself working through issues slower because it is easier to avoid them when no one is checking up on you. Nevertheless, if you remain committed to your recovery, success using unguided self-therapy is indeed possible.

One-On-One Therapy

Talk therapy is incredibly beneficial for individuals who need the support and guidance of a professional as they embark on their recovery journey. No matter whether it is CBT, DBT, or standard one-on-one talk therapy to get through to the causes of a person's BED, working with a therapist can provide people with the support they need. It is especially beneficial for those who have tried the self-help route but find themselves dropping off from the program because it is too difficult to face their demons. Having someone coaching you through these programs can help you stick to them, knowing that they believe in you.

Group Therapy

Group therapy is another beneficial approach for those who feel alone in their suffering with BED. The support and understanding that a person receives in a group setting can be incredibly beneficial in their recovery. The simple knowl-edge of not being the only person who suffers from BED and seeing how it can affect absolutely anyone can strengthen one's resolve to get the help they need to recover. Group therapy allows people to make friends and work through recovery programs together. In this way, they can hold each other accountable and be each other's strength when they need to.

These different types of therapy ensure that people can find one that is most suit-able for their comfort levels. Even more accommodating is the fact that therapy sessions can happen in person or online. Online sessions sometimes make it easier for people to talk, giving them a sense of safety of being in a place of familiarity. It can be a game changer for people who are shy or take time to get comfortable with others, even if they are medical professionals.

Medication

Treatment for BED using medication is possible. However, it all depends on your medical history. If you have existing comorbidities, such as depression or OCD, you may be given medication to manage those disorders that will help with your BED. There is currently only one medication that is approved by the Food and Drug Administration (FDA) and that is Lisdexamfetamine. This drug is commonly used to treat attention-deficit hyperactivity disorder (ADHD) but has been shown to help adults treat BED successfully. Although effective, it can have some nasty side effects such as insomnia and an elevated heart rate. Also, it can become problematic due to its addictive nature and is, therefore, unsuitable for those who have a history of substance abuse (Bothwell, 2022). It is due to these reasons that it is only prescribed as a last resort should no other treatment options work.

Nutrition Counseling

Working closely with a dietician is also recommended to treat BED. It is not about weight gain or weight loss but instead focuses on healing your perspective of food. One of the crucial factors of nutrition counseling is helping people with BED replace their BED beliefs about food with cold hard facts. This helps them to recognize their distorted thoughts and learn more about their nutritional needs. No two people have the same requirements and this results in personalized strategies being developed. In addition, working with a dietician can eradicate restrictive diets which may be a major contributor to a person's BED.

It is not uncommon for all of these treatments to be used in some form when seeking professional help. It can be overwhelming working with a therapist, medical doctor, and dietician. However, due to the complexity of BED, it is best that there is a holistic approach to treatment that focuses on treating all aspects of the disorder. It also helps to have a personal perspective that can determine which is the best approach. Some people may have better results from nutrition counseling than with guided therapy while others may do best with only medication. You can only find the right one for you if you take action and explore various options.

The Power of Self-Care

The term "self-care" has been thrown around a lot in recent years. It also has the unfortunate reputation of being a selfish pastime. However, self-care is anything but selfish as it is a pivotal part of our overall health and well-being. If we do not look after ourselves, how can we make a meaningful contribution to the lives of others? We first have to take care of ourselves, and for people recovering from BED, self-care is an important component of getting better. BED is associated with low self-esteem, negative self-image, and poor self-confidence.

As you begin your journey to recovery, you will soon find that not only your relationship with food will change, but also your relationship with yourself. Prioritizing self-care as you proceed with your recovery and even afterward will help you take control of your life and prioritize your well-being.

Workbook Activity: Strategy #1—Managing Your Expectations

Now that we have learned all about the treatment options for BED, it's time to look at our first actionable strategy for your journey to recovery. This strategy is all about managing the expectations you have about your recovery. You need to have the right mindset and avoid high expectations that will set you up for failure. To ensure that you have the right expectations, you should set realistic goals right from the start. So, let's go through what you need to do step-by-step.

Success does not happen with one event. It happens as a result of many small steps one takes to achieve their desired outcome. Every day take one small step and watch the magic happen -Kathleen Cage

Step 1: Goal Identification

The first step is to identify the specific areas you want to work on regarding your BED. These will be the areas that you set goals within. Take your time and consider all the aspects you would like to work on. The best way to determine these specific areas is by reviewing your responses to Steps 1 through 6 in Chapter 3 under Mapping Your BED Cycle in the Workbook Activity.

Some examples could be:

- improving your relationship with food
- emotional well-being
- improving self-care
- personal growth

Step 2: SMART Goal Setting

You may have heard of Specific, Measurable, Achievable, Relevant, and Time-bound (SMART) goals before in the workplace. However, smart goals can be used in all areas of your life, including your BED recovery. Thus, you need to ensure that your goals are specific and have ways in which you can track and measure them. Furthermore, they must be achievable and not too big for you to handle, they need to be relevant to your recovery and have a date by which they need to be achieved. If you set your goals in this manner, you have a clear path and timeline to follow.

Step 3: Clarify Your Goals

Once you have a list of your goals, answer the following questions for <u>each</u> of them. Through this process, you will achieve a more profound comprehension of your objectives, ultimately attaining clarity and infusing them with significance.

- What is your desired outcome regarding this goal? Is it a specific behavior or result?

_____

_____

_____

_____

- How will you measure your progress when pursuing this goal? What are the milestones or indicators that will signify your progress?

_____

_____

_____

_____

- Consider your current circumstances. Is this goal achievable considering your current resources and support system?

_____

_____

_____

_____

- Does this goal align with your BED recovery journey and does it contribute to your overall well-being?

_____

_____

_____

_____

- What are the specific steps or actions that you need to take to work toward this goal?

_____

_____

_____

_____

- Do you anticipate any potential challenges or obstacles when pursuing this goal? What can you do to overcome them?

_____

_____

_____

_____

- If you positively achieve this goal, how will it impact your recovery from BED and your life as a whole?

_____

_____

_____

_____

- Can you think of any specific strategies, techniques, or tools you can use to support your progress?

_____

_____

_____

_____

- When you achieve this goal, how will you celebrate or reward yourself?

_____

_____

_____

_____

- Does this goal align with the vision you have for your life in the future? What about your values?

_____

_____

_____

_____

Step 4: Action Plan

Using the answers to the questions in Step 3, put together an action plan for each goal you have identified. You need to do this by breaking down your goals into smaller steps that are easier to manage. In addition, you must also assign deadlines for you to achieve each step.

_____

_____

_____

_____

_____

_____

Step 5: Commitment and Accountability

You need to commit to your goals and hold yourself accountable for your progress. However, you should also consider sharing these goals with your therapist, support group, or a friend whom you trust to hold you accountable and provide support along the way.

These five steps will help you set realistic goals regarding your recovery. They will help you manage your expectations by giving you a clear path to follow, with defined tasks that need to be completed within a specific timeline, leaving no room for confusion. You need to remember that recovery from BED takes time and progress may not always be as straightforward as you anticipate. Remain compassionate with yourself throughout this journey and remember to celebrate the wins, learn from your losses, and adapt your goals with what you learn along the way.

You would think that taking tiny little steps would seem so trivial. Not true! It is better to take many small steps in the right direction, than none at all. Keep moving and you will pass obstacles that have defeated you before. Even if you don't see results right away, don't give up, because every small step you make towards that goal is affecting you in ways you would never imagine. -Brigitte Nicole

Reflective Questions

Here are some questions that will help you reflect on what we have discussed in this chapter and that will help you set up your journey to recovery.

- What are the specific goals you have identified for your emotional well-being during your BED recovery?

_____

_____

_____

- Have you considered how you will measure your progress toward improving your relationship with food?

_____

_____

_____

- Have you included achievable goals regarding your self-care that will support your recovery? What are they?

_____

_____

_____

- How will your personal growth contribute to your recovery from BED?

_____

_____

_____

- Can you identify ways to implement mindfulness into your daily routines in a way that will support achieving your goals?

_____

_____

_____

- How will achieving your goals improve your health, well-being, and overall quality of life?

_____

_____

_____

- What resources have you identified that will help you in your recovery?

_____

_____

_____

- How will these goals contribute to your visions of a binge-free future and a healthier relationship with food and yourself?

_____

_____

_____

Overcoming BED is indeed possible. You have a variety of treatment options available and it is just a matter of having the right intentions, goals, and mindset to commit to your recovery. We have covered the first strategy of managing your expectations by setting realistic goals in this chapter. Next, we will look at how you can develop a growth mindset that will help you overcome challenges along your journey to recovery.

YOUR INSIGHT CAN ILLUMINATE PATHS!

Hello, my friend,

As you navigate the chapters of 'A Roadmap to Recovery: Overcoming Binge Eating Disorder,' remember that your journey transcends the pages you turn. It's a voyage of understanding, with each chapter marking a significant milestone. This book serves as your vessel, carrying the valuable cargo of your experiences. The insights you gain are not just for you; they illuminate the path for others embarking on this challenging journey for the first time, offering them a guiding light and a roadmap to find their way through the darkness.

Your experiences, as unique and deeply personal as they are, hold immense value—not just for you, but for the community of individuals who are on similar paths but may not have come as far. Have you ever considered the power of shared experience? How your story, your insights, and your reflections could serve as a beacon of hope for someone else?

Sharing a review is a generous act of empathy. It's a way to tell someone else, "I've been there, and there is a way through." You don't need to have all the answers, nor do you need to be at the end of your journey. What matters is the honesty and the connection your unique perspective can forge.

I invite you to share your voice because it is indispensable. Picture another reader, perhaps feeling uncertain and looking for guidance. Your review could be the very thing that helps them take the next step forward.

With this invitation to share your insights, I hope to cultivate a community where empathy and support are paramount. Your words can make a profound difference in someone's life, and I look forward to seeing the light you can bring to those still finding their way. Let's make every word count toward lighting the path to recovery and understanding.

I made it simple for you to share your thoughts and reflections. All you need to do is visit *https://www.Amazon.com/review/create-review? &asin=B0D32BJDMF* or scan this QR code:

(you may need to sign in to your Amazon account)

There, you can recount what has touched you, the insights you've gained, and the moments that have stayed with you. Your honesty will light the way for someone else in need of guidance.

Your words have more power than you might realize. They can comfort, inspire, and validate the experiences of others. Your review is a small yet significant way to extend support to a community of readers who may be seeking just the kind of wisdom and encouragement you can offer.

So please, take a moment to share your journey thus far. Leave a review, not just as feedback for myself, but as a lifeline for others. Your voice is not just powerful; it's needed.

Your empathy. Your impact. Our shared path to recovery.

CHAPTER 5

ADDRESSING CONCERNS—OVERCOMING HURDLES ON THE PATH TO RECOVERY

Our greatest glory is not in never failing, but in rising every time we fail

— CONFUCIUS

Throughout our lives, we can expect to experience highs and lows. It is not possible to avoid the lows, and without them, we wouldn't appreciate the highs. The path to recovery from BED is no different. You cannot expect it to be a smooth road without any bumps—nothing is that easy.

However, what you can expect is to learn from the bumps on your recovery journey and use your newfound knowledge to navigate this road more easily. Sure, there will be frustration, irritation, and sometimes even disappointment, but what there should never be is a sense of failure. For this to happen, you need to have the right mindset during your recovery—which is what this chapter will help you with.

Strategy #2: Embracing a Growth Mindset

The concept of a growth mindset is not new. It is largely used in the workplace or even in school settings as they try to teach children about resilience. It was first introduced by Carol Dweck in 2006 and was used to describe the mindset of individuals who continue to learn and grow throughout their lives. On the flip side, those individuals with a fixed mindset believe that their intelligence is a fixed trait that cannot be altered. You can probably already tell from this description that people with fixed mindsets limit themselves and their abilities.

However, it's not just about how much you can learn in your lifetime. Having a growth mindset can be a powerful tool that can help you in your personal and professional life. In particular, when considering your BED recovery, a growth mindset is exactly what you need to overcome the hurdles you may experience. Let's take a closer look at how a growth mindset can help you.

Why is a Growth Mindset Important for Your Recovery?

A lot of people might wonder how a growth mindset will help in their BED recovery. How does believing that you can continue to learn and grow make you find relief from binge eating? Well, let me explain.

Allows You to Embrace Change

A growth mindset will help you embrace the changes in your life that will occur during your BED recovery. Often, when we are stuck in a BED cycle, the thought of any changes can be daunting. Even though we know that binge eating is bad, the thought of stepping out of our "comfort zone" and admitting our secret shame is scary and intimidating. Furthermore, the changes that we have to implement during our recovery process can also seem threatening.

However, if you have a growth mindset, you can learn to embrace change because it teaches you to embrace change as an opportunity for growth. Change is not scary with a growth mindset because you shift your thinking away from what will be different and focus instead on what will be better in your life. This subtle shift can make a world of difference in how you view and pursue your recovery.

Drives Lifelong Learning

Not only does having a growth mindset benefit your recovery process, but it also drives a habit of lifelong learning. This ensures that even after you have overcome your BED, you can continue to learn and maintain your healthy lifestyle. You will find new ways to handle challenging situations, be able to overcome setbacks and adapt your approach to maintaining your recovery if needed.

Furthermore, if you are always learning new skills, you will always be growing and, therefore, will always be the best possible version of yourself. If you don't know something, you will embrace it as something that you will have to learn and not something that you lack.

Inspires Positive Results

When you have a growth mindset, success is not a question because you know you will succeed—it is just a matter of when you will succeed. A growth mindset inspires positive results because it focuses on positive outcomes. It's not a matter of being eternally optimistic, but rather understanding that success is possible with hard work and commitment. You know that no matter what comes your way, you will figure out a way to overcome it. It might delay your progress but it does not halt your recovery in any way.

Builds Resilience

Resilience is the ability to bounce back from setbacks. A growth mindset helps to build resilience because you know that a setback is not a failure. Being resilient in your BED recovery—and beyond—is a crucial skill that will allow you to persevere in the face of adversity. There is no such thing as a failure because it is an opportunity to learn from a setback and adapt your approach. Thus, you will not be tempted to quit your journey altogether because you know you just have to re-evaluate and map out a new path.

Helps You Learn From Mistakes

A common occurrence amongst BED sufferers is that once we slip up in our recovery or diet attempts, we completely fall off the wagon. Our mistake, or inability to follow through, tells us that we can't do it. However, with a growth mindset, we see our mistakes as an opportunity to learn. We will try to figure out why things didn't work out and how we can continue on our journey without making the same mistake again. This fosters continued learning, resilience, adaptability, and progress—all of which are great life skills to have.

These five factors demonstrate how valuable a growth mindset can be in your BED recovery. It may seem far-fetched, but it's really as simple as changing the way you perceive learning and opportunities to learn. With a growth mindset, you open up a world of possibilities that not only inspires your BED recovery but ensures it.

How to Embrace a Growth Mindset

Knowing the importance of a growth mindset is crucial, but you also have to learn how to embrace it. To cultivate a growth mindset, you have to shift your perspectives on learning and embrace new ways of dealing with different situations in life. It won't just help your recovery progress, it will change your life for the better. Here's what you need to do.

Don't Identify Problems, Recognize Challenges

A simple way to embrace a growth mindset is to forget the word "problem." There are no problems in your recovery, only challenges. This simple change in vocabulary will automatically have you looking for ways to overcome your challenges instead of complaining or overthinking problems. When we have problems, we begin to question everything because it feels like the universe is against our progress.

In contrast, when you have challenges you know that they will test your resolve, but you also know that with time, you will be able to overcome them. Our words are powerful drivers of our thoughts, and changing our words can help ease the shift to a growth mindset.

Embrace the Good and Bad

Life is not perfect. There may be moments that feel perfect, but they don't last forever. If you accept this fact, you will not get derailed when something goes wrong or when faced with a difficult situation. You understand that it will pass with time and you just have to see how things play out. In most cases, we try too hard to control situations in an attempt to avoid the uncomfortableness that we experience. For people with BED, it can mean the onset of a binge eating episode.

However, if you begin to change how you think about these situations you can begin to embrace a growth mindset. This will enable you to work through difficult times. You just have to remember that it's only because of the presence of darkness that you can appreciate the light.

Practice Gratitude

Having an attitude of gratitude can change your mindset for the better. When you begin to appreciate things in your life, you think less about your hardships. Furthermore, when you start trying to identify what you can be grateful for in negative situations, you will realize that it's not as bad as it seems.

For example, let's consider a common situation where a person is unhappy with their body and the fact that it can't be like the perfect people they see on Instagram. Normally, this would trigger a pattern of negative thoughts that can lead to a binge eating episode. However, if you instead think of the fact that your body is healthy, serves you daily, and enables you to do whatever you need to, there is a chance that you will feel more content with your body.

Don't Be Afraid to Ask for Help

It's impossible to know everything. No matter how smart you are, there will always be something newly developed or discovered in the world that you might not be aware of. As much as the continuous pursuit of knowledge is great, you will not know everything—and that is okay. You have to be able to recognize that some things are beyond your scope and that it is okay to ask for help from others who have more experience than you.

For example, you may have tried to pursue your BED recovery before on your own and did not have much success. Reaching out to a professional who has extensive knowledge of the disorder and who can help guide and advise you may be what you need to overcome BED once and for all. Asking for help does not make you weak—it means that you know yourself well enough to know when help is necessary.

Set Goals

Setting goals is a great way to embrace a growth mindset because it gives you tangible targets to strive for. In having goals, you can work toward them; enhancing your skills and learning more in the process.

Furthermore, as you achieve your goals, you reinforce your growth mindset because you can see positive changes in your life that will motivate you to continue setting new goals in the future. This is how a growth mindset drives positive results in every aspect of your life, including your recovery.

Be Curious and Try New Things

When we were kids, our curiosity fueled our learning. We would ask questions, eagerly watch what intrigued us, and were determined to learn everything we could. As we get older and others begin to dictate how we should educate ourselves, we tend to lose this curiosity and passion to learn.

However, if we can tap into that curiosity again, we can easily cultivate a growth mindset as adults. Furthermore, when we are curious we want to try new things, which sparks new knowledge and leads to meeting new people. These all contribute to your growth as a person on a professional and personal level.

Learn From Failure

Past failures influence our future actions in many ways. A fear of failure can emerge, hindering us from making further attempts or deterring us from venturing beyond our comfort zone. However, if we shift our mindset to learning from our failures, it will strengthen our approach to future endeavors. It helps us learn what doesn't work and builds our problem-solving skills—both of which contribute to better approaches with better results.

Don't Resent Criticism

Not many people take criticism well—after all, someone is telling you what is wrong with you or that you didn't do something right. However, in most cases, the person is not doing it to be mean and tell you how bad you are at something. Instead, they are trying to communicate what can be done better and what you need to work toward improving. Thus, if ever in a position where you are receiving criticism, it is best to pause and evaluate what the person is saying. It could be constructive and could actually help you in the long run.

Embracing a growth mindset involves simple actions but they require conscious decisions. The good thing is that the more you implement these conscious decisions, the greater your chances of turning it into a habit. With this in mind, let's take a look at some specific circumstances in which you can use a growth mindset to aid your recovery from BED.

Navigating Limited Support: Building a Network

A support network is an important asset in everyone's life. Since BED is very much a lonely disorder because people often isolate themselves, a support system is an integral piece of the recovery process. Not only does having people supporting you help, but you will also find the presence and guidance of others can also be beneficial—especially if they have been in your position before.

This is where a growth mindset comes in handy, because it will not only help you understand that asking for help is okay, but also drive the need to build a diverse network that can be a multifaceted advantage in your recovery and life in general. People with BED may have difficulty building a network or even identifying who should be in their network depending on the severity of their disorder. In this section, we will cover the benefits of a support system and how to go about building one.

Benefits of a Social Support System

There are three main types of support systems one can have. These are an emotional support system, a social support system, and a professional support system. While each has its merit, a social support system is most robust as it has the potential to be all three systems in one if you have the right people in it. Here are the top five benefits of having such a system for your BED recovery.

Increases Resilience

Having a good social support group can increase your resilience when faced with difficult situations. As much as having a growth mindset can help you weather the storm on your own, a strong support network with people you can turn to for advice, motivation, and strength to continue, is a powerful tool. If your resilience ever wavers, your support network will help steady you and allow you to continue your path of recovery.

Better Overall Health

If you have people you can lean on in times of difficulty, you are generally physically, mentally, and emotionally stronger. It improves your overall health by decreasing anxiety and anxiety-related issues like high blood pressure, cardiovascular disease, and depression.

Furthermore, a good social support system consists of people who know you well and may be able to identify issues regarding your health before you even notice them. This helps you stay healthy and avoid any setbacks as you pursue your recovery journey.

Provide Valuable Guidance

A well-built social support group consists of diverse people with different life experiences—with some of them possibly recovering from an eating disorder as well. Because of this, they can provide valuable guidance to those suffering from BED and help them see things from different perspectives. It provides valuable insight and can help you work through blind spots that you have missed.

Enhance Wins and Decrease Losses

When you have a solid support network, it is possible to celebrate wins together and evaluate the losses. In doing so, your wins are enhanced as multiple people celebrate your progress and motivate you to continue.

On the flip side, your losses won't seem as bad when your support network comes together to lift your spirits and remind you of your end goal. Furthermore, when there are so many people involved, they can help you evaluate your setbacks and plan new approaches.

Improved Mental Health

Having a good support network can be just as efficient as having a therapist. They help to lift you up when you are down and remind you of what is important when you get thrown off course. One of the best ways that a support group improves your mental health is by helping you see yourself clearly when your thoughts are distorted. Far too often, people are thrown off their path of recovery because their mental health takes a hit. However, if you have the right people in your support system, they will act as your compass and bring you back to where you need to be.

How to Build a Social Support System

Sometimes, building a social support system can be difficult. You know that you should reach out to people, but you may be unsure as to who. In addition, you may have already isolated yourself from your friends and family and find it challenging to start nurturing those relationships again. I know how you feel because I have been in this very spot before. This is why I wanted to take you through some of the ways you can go about building your social support system to help you on your recovery journey.

Join a Support Group

The best and quickest way to build a social support system is to join a support group. Not only will you meet people who understand what you are going through, but everyone in the group is working toward their recovery. This provides a valuable network of diverse individuals whom you can talk to and gain valuable advice.

Furthermore, you might find that it is easier to open up to people who know what you are experiencing because they have experienced the same thing. Hearing stories from others will inspire you to share yours and everyone gains strength and confidence from each other.

Try Therapy

For some people, a therapist could be all the social support they need. Speaking to a professional is always a good idea. They can help you with your recovery process and they can also help you with other issues from your past that you have not yet dealt with. They can recognize patterns and behaviors in you that others may not be able to see due to their lack of expertise. In addition, a therapist gives objective advice which is something you may not always receive from friends and family members.

Use Online Resources

If you don't want to physically go to support group meetings or want support but wish to remain anonymous, you can use online resources to find anonymous support groups, chatrooms, and even online therapists or counselors. You will still gain the same valuable support and guidance without having to meet people face-to-face. This may be a more comfortable option for introverts or until a person builds up enough confidence to physically attend a group meeting or therapist session.

Think About Your Existing Networks

Most of us have existing networks in the form of friends, family members, colleagues, and even neighbors. You can identify the type of people you want in your support group—those who you trust, those that you know will be honest with you, and those who know you best. These are the people who bring out the best in you and improve your life with their presence. Having them with you on your recovery journey will not just make the journey easier but will also provide accountability because they are aware of what you want to achieve.

Do Things You Love

Meeting like-minded people who share the same interests as you do can spark powerful relationships. This is why going out and doing the things you love is crucial to meeting new people. These people can be valuable members of your support group because they don't judge your history. They come into your life and get to know you and your journey from your current perspective. This is something that is refreshing, as friends and family may sometimes know too much and be critical instead of supportive.

Volunteer

Volunteering in your community is an excellent way to meet people in the surrounding area. You will get to witness how they interact, help, and work with other people. This will give you an idea of how they will function within your support system and how they can help you. Working together to help others also builds kinship, boosts confidence, and gives you a sense of community that can improve your mood and bolster your resilience.

A social support system is an important part of your recovery and one that you should not take lightly. You must not be plagued by thoughts of who can't be in your support system or how they will feel being left out when someone else is included. Instead, you must carefully evaluate who has your trust, who is always honest with you, and who respects you. Furthermore, you must be comfortable with opening up to them as they will be a part of your most vulnerable moments. However, in doing so, you will be supported and always have people to lean on when you need it the most.

Dealing with Past Failures: Learning from Setbacks

Recovery from BED seems simple to people who have never experienced an eating disorder. They believe that it is just a matter of having a strict diet that you have to stick to and any failures are due to a lack of discipline. You and I both know that it's never so simple. Not only is focusing on a diet a surefire way of avoiding recovery but relapses are never due to lack of discipline—they are so much more complicated than that.

The journey to recovery is not a straight road and navigating setbacks is a crucial lesson that we must learn. A growth mindset encourages learning from setbacks in order to strengthen your approach as you continue on your journey. Having this way of thinking will allow you to continue on your path to recovery no matter how long it will take.

In fact, recovery from BED is indeed a long journey that consists of three definite parts (National Eating Disorders Association, 2018). There is the physical recovery from an eating disorder which looks at addressing any health consequences one may have suffered. These include addressing problems with weight, electrolyte balance, hormone imbalances, and nutrient levels, to name a few.

The second part is behavioral recovery whereby a person will have to address the actual behavior of binge eating. They will need to assess their behaviors and try to stop binge eating.

Lastly, there is psychological recovery which is undoubtedly the hardest part of recovery. This is where people address the reasons behind their binge eating and learn how to deal with them including working on any other mental issues that may be present.

Dealing with these three aspects of recovery takes time and you need to remain patient and present as you work through them. Rushing them or not completing them correctly will easily cause relapses as you fail to learn how to properly deal with each component. Other common reasons for relapses or setbacks in BED recovery include

- changes in weight
- social events
- hunger
- lack of self-care

These four occurrences can throw you off course from your recovery. They can seriously affect your thoughts about yourself and if you have not worked through the psychological aspects of your binge-eating properly, you do not stand a chance against them.

Therefore, it is essential that you know how to pick up signs that you are on the way to a relapse before it occurs. These signs are easy to recognize because you begin to slip into old habits that include negative thought patterns and behaviors. Being aware of this and forming ways of dealing with them can be the key to avoiding relapses.

However, you also need to be kind to yourself and realize that this is a part of the recovery process. It will take time until you get it right and overcome BED. Acceptance of setbacks and understanding the lessons they provide will only make you stronger.

Workbook Activity: Dealing With Setbacks During BED Recovery

Learning how to deal with setbacks during a recovery process is a personal journey. Everyone will have a particular cause for their setback and will need slightly different approaches to dealing with them. This workbook activity is designed to help you navigate this process. The questions asked will make you pause and carefully analyze your setback and its cause, allowing you to better understand how to continue moving forward on your recovery journey.

Use the space below to write down your answers or grab a pen and notebook if you want to get messy somewhere else!

- Think of a recent setback while working through your BED recovery. Describe what happened.

_____

_____

_____

_____

- Is it possible to identify the trigger that caused this setback? Was it a particular event, emotion, or circumstance?

_____

_____

_____

_____

- What was your initial response to this setback?

_____

_____

_____

_____

- Did you find the setback challenging? Why?

_____

_____

_____

_____

- Write down the negative thoughts and emotions that the setback brought about. How did these impact your motivation and confidence?

_____

_____

_____

_____

- Can you identify any patterns or themes that occurred prior to a setback? Can you find any common triggers of events?

_____

_____

_____

_____

- What lessons can you identify about this setback? Is there anything you learned about yourself that you didn't recognize before?

_____

_____

_____

_____

- Do you have any effective coping mechanisms in place that help you deal with setbacks? Did you use any of these coping mechanisms to deal with this setback?

_____

_____

_____

_____

- Do you have any unhealthy coping mechanisms or behaviors that need to be replaced?

_____

_____

_____

_____

- Looking back, can you identify three actionable steps you can take to overcome this setback and get back to your path to recovery?

_____

_____

_____

_____

- During setbacks, if you need support, who can you currently reach out to?

_____

_____

_____

_____

- Think about those negative thoughts and emotions again. How can you reframe these to develop a positive growth mindset?

_____

_____

_____

_____

- Forget about setbacks for a moment. Have you celebrated your progress and the success you have had on your recovery journey? If you have not, what can you do to acknowledge your achievements?

_____

_____

_____

_____

- Are there any self-care activities or practices that you can implement daily to boost your resilience and well-being during your recovery process?

_____

_____

_____

_____

- Moving forward, can you identify any potential challenges that may come up that will jeopardize your progress? What strategies can you put in place now to prepare for them?

_____

_____

_____

_____

Don't let thinking about your setbacks dampen your mood. It's important to think of setbacks as chances to learn and grow instead of failures. Your answers are crucial for developing an action plan for moving forward in your recovery journey. It is better to be proactive and have strategies in place now that will help you ensure positive outcomes in the future.

In the next chapter, we will go through the emotional aspects of recovery and how to develop healthy coping mechanisms to help ensure steady progress.

CHAPTER 6

EMOTIONAL TRIGGERS—TACKLING GUILT, SHAME, AND EMOTIONAL EATING

I intend to accept my body today, love my body
tomorrow, and appreciate my body always.

—ANONYMOUS

A large part of a BED recovery is dealing with the emotional triggers that are associated with it. We have touched on these emotions previously but the guilt and shame that come with a binge-eating episode can be debilitating. Learning what to do when these emotions hit can be the difference between recovery and relapse for most people with BED. In this chapter, we will cover how to deal with the guilt and shame associated with BED by developing emotional awareness and healthy coping strategies.

Dealing With Guilt and Shame

If you have tried recovering from your BED before, you are well aware of the guilt that washes over you when you slip up. It is overpowering, and the thoughts that flood your mind fill you with shame. This is when your mental barrier is at its lowest and the attacks come from your own thoughts, beating you down even further. As a result, a relapse is more than likely to occur because your BED cycle has been reactivated. Once this happens, the guilt and shame build up again and continue to strengthen the cycle because we make no attempt to counter these emotions. Even though it hurts us, we don't have the strength to go against them and this further worsens the way we feel toward ourselves.

I want you to know that it is indeed possible to overcome this guilt. It has nothing to do with willpower or strength. Instead, it has to do with mindset, emotional awareness, and knowing how to speak to yourself.

Here are some valuable tips regarding dealing with guilt and shame.

Forgive Yourself

The first thing you should do if you slip up during your recovery is to forgive yourself. You are only human and are bound to make mistakes. Furthermore, life is not perfect, and setbacks will occur whether you like it or not. Therefore, it is not constructive to focus on what a failure you are and how you should have prevented it from happening, because you are not a failure! Setbacks are a part of life. It's what you do to move forward from it that counts. So, forgive yourself for what is already done and shift your focus to what you will do to get back on your path to recovery.

Forget About Punishments

One of the first reactions to our guilt is to try and punish ourselves or find some way to compensate for our actions. This could be in the form of a more rigorous exercise plan, cutting back calories, or even skipping meals. None of these are going to make you feel better. In fact, we have already discussed how restrictive diets work in feeding BED cycles. Thus, you will end up doing more harm than good and trigger even more feelings of guilt and shame. You can't punish yourself for slipping up because it does not make sense to punish yourself for being human. It's like deciding you don't deserve the vacation you planned because you made a wrong turn!

Analyze What Happened

When feelings of guilt and shame hit, instead of wallowing in it, you must aim to use it as a trigger to activate your curiosity and investigative skills. This will help you to analyze what caused you to deviate from your recovery. You can use it as an opportunity to develop and grow your growth mindset as you look for the cause and figure out ways to adapt your future approaches to avoid the same pitfalls. It also will serve as a productive distraction, providing a way to process the guilt and shame before they affect you any further.

Challenge Your Thoughts

Most of the thoughts that arise alongside feelings of guilt and shame are false and unkind. They tear us down and make us forget all about the progress we have made. If you learn to challenge these thoughts and reframe them into more positive thinking patterns, you can change the trajectory of your potential relapse.

For example, if you start to think you're a failure, immediately fill your mind with the progress you have made. If you start to feel like you should continue bingeing because you have already fallen off the wagon, think about how good it will feel when you overcome the shackles of your BED. These distorted thoughts must not get the best of you and reframing them is a healthy habit to build.

Take a Time Out

Removing yourself from your immediate environment and finding ways to relax can also help you deal with feelings of guilt and shame. It prevents you from staying in the same place and feeling the same things by providing a distraction and calming activity. Spending time in nature can be particularly helpful in grounding yourself and remembering to stay on your path to recovery. Just ensure that whatever you do takes you outside the house and allows your brain to shake the intrusive and distorted thoughts.

Get Professional Help

Reaching out to a professional to discuss what you are going through can be a liberating experience. Not only can they provide valuable advice, but they also provide a safe space for you to voice your emotions. This is a way to process your guilt and shame, allowing it to run its course with the guidance of a professional. You will also be able to gain a deeper understanding of why these emotions have a hold on you and learn how to deal with them on your own.

These emotions must not be allowed to pull you back into a BED cycle. If you can effectively deal with them when they arise, you can grow your resilience and continue pursuing your recovery. An integral part of dealing with these emotions is developing your emotional awareness—which is what we will cover next.

Strategy #3: Developing Emotional Awareness

People with BED know that emotions are powerful drivers of the disorder. We binge to escape our emotions—to not feel anything that makes us uncomfortable with ourselves. The fact that this occurs means that we are not good at regulating our emotions. Emotional awareness and regulation are actions that we begin to develop in childhood. If we do not learn to regulate our emotions effectively when we are young, we struggle when we are older. Our responses to our emotions may seem exaggerated, resulting in severe mood swings, poor decisions, difficulty communicating, and strained relationships. Therefore, an inability to regulate emotions affects all aspects of our lives and we miss out on valuable moments because our emotions get the best of us.

To be able to regulate our emotions properly, we require emotional awareness. When we are aware of our emotions, we can not only recognize our emotions when they arise, but we can also understand ourselves and our actions better. The more we know ourselves, the better we can navigate difficult situations and recognize emotional reactions in others. It is a powerful skill and one that can be learned at any time. With emotional awareness, you get a better understanding of your likes and dislikes, what triggers your actions, and what drives your decisions. This empowers us not only in our BED recovery but also in our daily lives by preventing our emotions from overwhelming us.

Evaluating Your Emotional Awareness

Before you work on developing this skill, you must first evaluate your current levels of emotional awareness. This will give you a better idea of what you need to focus on. To evaluate your current levels of emotional awareness, you need to ask yourself a series of reflective questions. So, grab your notebooks or use the space provided below to answer the following questions.

- Consider strong emotions such as anger, fear, joy, and sadness. How do you react to them? Can you tolerate them in yourself and others?

_____

_____

_____

- Do you experience physical reactions to emotions? Think about when you are angry or sad—is there a physical sensation that accompanies these emotions?

_____

_____

_____

- Do your emotions guide your decisions? Will you do something based on a gut feeling?

_____

_____

_____

- Do you trust your intuition in different situations? For example, if you get goosebumps when entering a building, do you believe that there is something wrong?

_____

_____

_____

- How comfortable are you with your emotions? Do you express them freely or do you try to suppress them? Do you pass judgment on yourself for having them?

_____

_____

_____

- Do you notice the change in your emotions throughout the day or do you only register large fluctuations?

_____

_____

_____

- How comfortable are you talking about your emotions? Do you find it easy to communicate your feelings honestly to others?

_____

_____

_____

- Do you feel that other people understand your emotions? Are you comfortable with others knowing your emotions at all?

_____

_____

_____

- Can you pick up what other people are feeling?   Are you able to empathize with others and be sensitive to their emotions?

_____

_____

_____

The answers to these questions should give you an idea of how emotionally aware you really are. To be fair, most of us have very little emotional awareness. It's not because we are unfeeling robots, but more that very few of us are asked to evaluate our feelings growing up. It's just not something that people think about until they are asked to.

When you lack emotional awareness, you lack the ability to manage your emotions effectively. As a result, you will avoid emotions altogether to avoid inappropriate actions. However, what happens when you avoid emotions you perceive as negative is that you end up avoiding positive emotions as well. Emotional awareness gives you the tools needed to manage your emotions and lead a happier and more fulfilling life.

How to Improve Emotional Awareness

Improving your emotional awareness takes time and patience. It involves a lot of self-reflection, careful analysis, and commitment—but it is definitely worth it. Once you improve your emotional awareness, you will begin to see how different your personal and professional life can be.

More importantly, once you increase your emotional awareness, your BED recovery journey will also improve drastically. You will have fewer setbacks due to overwhelming emotions and you will be able to set realistic goals because you will know how your emotions, behaviors, and actions will contribute to achieving them. Here are some great ways you can work toward improving your emotional awareness and overall emotional intelligence.

Learn to Label Your Emotions

Many of us don't know our own emotions. How many times have you had a feeling but instead of saying what it was, you described it? This is actually a common occurrence. People unconsciously describe a feeling but don't name it.

For example, how many times have you heard people say they feel irritated but what they actually mean is angry? Irritation is not an emotion—anger is. The sooner we learn to label our emotions, the better equipped we are to recognize them correctly.

Mindfulness

The first step to building emotional awareness is to practice mindfulness. It allows you to start recognizing your emotions. When you are mindful of how you are feeling, you can better process your emotions before you act. This prevents your emotions from overwhelming you.

Furthermore, when you are mindful of the present moment, you can also analyze the situation better. This will ensure that you do not overreact and that the right emotion manifests.

Question Your Emotions

A great way to build emotional awareness is to question your emotions once you can identify them correctly. This not only provides you with more information about your emotions but helps you pause to understand and process them better. Here are some examples of questions to ask:

- What happened to make me feel this emotion? Was it an event, person, or something that stirred my senses?
- How does my body feel in response to this emotion?
- Was my body language affected by this emotion? How so?
- How did I act in response to this emotion?
- Was this emotion intense or overwhelming in any way?

Using your Journal

Using your journal to document your emotions can be extremely helpful. It allows you to work in the moment and write down the emotion, what caused it, and how you acted as a result of it. This prevents you from forgetting any details later on when you try to recall what happened.

Your journal is also helpful to process your emotions healthily. By writing it down, you accept it and let it run its course. Writing down your emotions also gives you the opportunity to reflect and learn from different situations so that your actions can improve in the future.

Practice Active Listening

Developing emotional awareness also entails being able to recognize the emotions of others. To do this, you need to be observant and practice active listening. This means that you should pay attention when others are talking. Too often, when someone else speaks, we focus on how we will respond and don't listen to the other person.

By taking the time to actively listen when someone speaks, you will be able to pick up on vocal and non-vocal cues that will indicate how they are feeling. Therefore, you will be able to communicate with empathy and strengthen your personal and professional relationships.

Put Yourself in Another's Shoes

Being able to empathize with others is also another way to develop emotional awareness. By putting yourself in somebody else's shoes and trying to understand where they are coming from, you can better understand emotions and how they affect our behaviors and actions. In addition, when you try to understand how another person is feeling, you are opening yourself up to different perspectives and growing as an individual.

Stop Complaining

A large portion of being emotionally unaware involves complaining. When a person cannot understand their emotions and what causes them, they often feel like the victim. They may constantly blame others for evoking their anger or making them feel sad. However, the emotion probably has nothing to do with the other person and more to do with our past experiences. Until we stop complaining and start asking questions about where the emotion is coming from, we will continue being victims of our emotions.

Improving your emotional awareness involves pausing to question your emotions and evaluating if they are justified or whether they are simply reactions brought about by past experiences. Being mindful, listening to yourself and others, and being curious about your emotions will drive your emotional awareness.

Practicing Self-Compassion

If we see our friends going through a difficult time, it is easy for us to show compassion. We want to see them get through whatever setback they have, and we encourage them, hoping that it makes them feel better. However, when it comes to giving ourselves the same treatment, it seems almost impossible. Self-compassion does not mean that you're feeling sorry for yourself—it just means that you understand that bad things happen and you are kind to yourself. This is easier said than done for most of us as we often resort to self-criticism and self-pity instead.

Practicing self-compassion can be the answer to breaking the shame and guilt associated with BED cycles. If we learn to show ourselves the compassion we share with others, it becomes easier to deal with setbacks. We will be more inclined to forgive and motivate ourselves to move on than to criticize our actions and fall back into old habits. This is why it is crucial that self-compassion be one of the skills you develop to aid you in your recovery.

The Benefits of Self-Compassion

Self-compassion has been proven to aid in the recovery of eating disorders (Kelly & Carter, 2014). However, this is not the only benefit of self-compassion. Here are the other reasons why you should be practicing self-compassion daily.

Self-compassion can

- improve your self-esteem
- help you have better relationships
- improve your performance at work or school
- help to build resilience
- prevents anxiety and depression
- increase happiness

These are just the main benefits of self-compassion. The more you practice it in your life, the easier it will become to live a healthier, happier life, free from self-criticism. You can shed the negativity that weighs you down and continue your recovery with self-compassion and understanding.

How to Practice Self-Compassion

Practicing self-compassion is something that you should do every day until it becomes a well-established habit. It's not a matter of being weak when you need discipline, or making excuses for your actions. Self-compassion is simply treating yourself as you would others who are going through the same situation.

Here's what you must aim to do to practice self-compassion:

- **Let Go of Perfection:** We have discussed the idea of perfection before—it does not exist. The sooner you let go of perfection, the better it will be to accept that setbacks will happen. We are only human and we each have weaknesses. If you accept this simple fact, you can be kinder to yourself and know that there is nothing wrong with you.

- **Ease Up on the Judgment:** It is not uncommon to judge yourself daily. Even saying or thinking "I'm so stupid," in jest is a form of judgment. You need to be mindful of these thoughts. Every time they occur, you need to stop and think if it is true or if you are being critical of yourself. It is never right to assume anything about anyone—including yourself.

- **Practice Forgiveness:** Let go of the past, your mistakes, and previous setbacks in your recovery. Forgiveness will set you free from the burden of guilt and shame. Forgive yourself and set your sights on what is happening currently. Stay focused on the present and take each day as it comes.

- **Find Your Sense of Self:** A large part of practicing self-compassion is becoming your own best friend. You need to speak to yourself as you would your best friend and as you do this, you will get to know yourself better. It may seem strange, but it really does work. You will learn more about yourself in your recovery journey than ever expected, and practicing self-compassion further enhances this.

Strategy #4: Cultivating Healthy Coping Strategies

Developing emotional awareness and practicing self-compassion are crucial steps to dealing with the emotional triggers associated with BED. Another excellent strategy to implement is healthy coping mechanisms. Whether we are aware of it or not, all of us have coping mechanisms—our BED is an example of that. If we cultivate healthy coping mechanisms, it can aid our recovery immensely by providing ways to process our emotions, avoid being self-critical, and focus on our path to overall health and wellness. This is why it is the fourth strategy that you must implement on your recovery journey.

The Purpose of Coping Strategies

Coping strategies or mechanisms provide ways in which a person can deal with a stressful or difficult event or emotion. They serve as outlets to process these situations and can be healthy or unhealthy. Healthy coping strategies occur when a person is aware of the situation that is causing them difficulty and they take steps to actively reduce the impact it has. Unhealthy coping mechanisms occur when someone uses an activity to avoid or hide from the problems they are faced with. Ideally, we need to cultivate healthy coping strategies to ensure that we don't avoid processing our emotions effectively during our recovery.

Research has shown that healthy coping strategies can be divided into four main categories (Algorani & Gupta, 2022). These are:

- Problem-focused strategies whereby an individual uses problem-solving strategies to deal with a situation.
- Emotion-focused strategies involve reframing negative thoughts with more positive ones.
- Social coping strategies whereby people seek support from their social network.
- Meaning-focused strategies are similar to growth mindset activities whereby an individual tries to find meaning in their difficult situation which, in turn, alleviates any stress or negative emotions.

Developing healthy coping strategies that encompass these four categories will provide a solid foundation for effectively handling your emotions during your

BED recovery and beyond. They become good habits that improve your overall health and wellness.

Healthy Coping Strategies to Try

Finding healthy coping strategies can very much be a personal experience. Knowing which strategies will work and which will function as a new way to avoid your problems instead of processing them takes a bit of trial and error. It will take time, but when you have them in place, you will be glad you took the time to choose the right ones. Here are some great options to try.

Guided Imagery

Guided imagery is a form of therapy whereby patients are asked to think of positive images of their future. A professional helps them hold on to this image and gain peace and comfort from it. In this way, guided imagery is a relaxation technique that helps remove the stress of a current situation and will help you focus on what a successful recovery from BED looks like.

Spend Time Outdoors

Spending time in nature has a calming effect on most people. It is an excellent way to step away from a stressful situation and settle your thoughts. The change of scenery may help to break the intense hold emotions can have on us and the fresh air will do wonders to clear your mind and allow you to process your emotions.

Be Creative

Artistic pursuits can be a great coping strategy. They provide an outlet for your emotions and give you time to process them. It is much healthier to throw some paint on a canvas than it is to throw a tantrum!

Deep Breathing

Focusing on your breathing is also a way to calm your mind and prevent emotions from taking over. It is an age-old technique that proves quite useful in driving mindfulness and relaxation. When you focus on breathing deeply, you bring your focus back to the present moment and prevent impulsive actions that you will regret later.

Meditation

Another mindfulness technique, meditation is a healthy coping strategy for everyone. When you are stressed or when your emotions threaten to overwhelm you, meditation can help you focus on what is important and help you reign in your emotions. It is also a great way to ensure that you make sound decisions and not impulsive ones that are merely reactions to your emotions. You can also use meditation in combination with what you learn from guided imagery to help strengthen your motivation toward recovery.

Exercise

Any form of exercise is a great coping strategy. Not only does it benefit your physical health, but it also allows you to improve your mental health as well. You can use exercise as an outlet for negative emotions and gain clarity when you need it the most.

Journaling

Writing in your journal, as we discussed earlier, is a very good way to process your thoughts and emotions healthily. Not only does writing them down provide an outlet, but it also allows you to evaluate your emotions and regulate them. You will find that writing them down will give you the ideal opportunity to reflect on your emotions and recognize where they are coming from. You can also always go back to your journal when you need to reflect on your actions and behaviors.

Seek Support

Seeking support from your nearest and dearest can help you process your emotions and deal with how you are feeling. It is healthy to talk to someone to voice your concerns, worries, and emotions. Through talking, you may even be able to find solutions or formulate action plans that will keep you on track to achieve your goals.

Taking a Bath/Shower

Sometimes all you need to process your thoughts and emotions is to have a shower or take a bath. It is a simple coping mechanism, but one that is extremely effective. Your body almost resets as you wash off the tension and step out with a clearer vision of how to move forward.

Many of the healthy coping strategies listed above have also been mentioned previously when we have discussed processing your emotions and embracing a growth mindset. This is because they work together to bring about all these wonderful changes to your life that will aid in your BED recovery. Be patient with yourself and work on developing healthy coping strategies that work for you. They might be a variation of what you are already doing, or they might be something entirely new. Whatever the case, take your time and keep trying strategies until you find the best strategies for you.

Workbook Activity: Crafting Your Personalized Healthy Coping Strategies for Binge Eating

The following activity will help you begin crafting your healthy coping strategies. It consists of a series of questions that you will need to answer to gauge what your coping strategies should consist of. Your answers can be as long or short as you like—as long as you are honest and committed to getting the information you need. You can use the space provided after each question below or use a separate notebook answer if you think you will need more space. Take your time and answer thoughtfully. Let's get started.

Questions

- Do you have any hobbies or participate in any activities that help you experience a sense of calm or joy?

_____

_____

_____

- Is it possible to incorporate these hobbies or activities into your daily or weekly routines?

_____

_____

_____

- Have you tried relaxation techniques such as guided imagery, progressive muscle relaxation, or deep breathing? If yes, have they been helpful?

_____

_____

_____

_____

- How can you use these relaxation techniques daily during times of stress or when your emotions threaten to overwhelm you?

_____

_____

_____

- What about physical activities or exercise? Do you enjoy them? Have you already incorporated them into your daily or weekly routines? If not, have you tried using them as an outlet to process your emotions?

_____

_____

_____

- Have you pursued any creative outlets before such as painting, playing a musical instrument, dancing, or writing? How can you make time for these activities?

_____

_____

_____

_____

- Do you have a support system in place that you can easily reach out to when needed?

_____

_____

_____

_____

- How can you incorporate self-care practices into your daily life so that they are not pushed aside?

_____

_____

_____

_____

- Are there any self-care practices that you feel particularly comforted by?

_____

_____

_____

_____

- Are there any challenges that you foresee with your recovery journey? How can you proactively implement coping strategies to help get you through this? Which coping strategies would work best for these challenges?

_____

_____

_____

_____

Actionable Steps

1. Review your answers above and identify the top three coping strategies that you feel will work best. Write these in your journal and make them prominent so to ensure your consistent focus and practice.
2. Integrate these coping strategies into your daily and weekly schedules.
3. Use reminders, alarms, or even an app to help you stick to these schedules and remain committed to following through on these coping strategies.

4. Share your action plan with your support system, therapist, or family so that you can be held accountable and receive support as you implement these strategies.

5. Monitor the effectiveness of the coping strategies you have chosen to implement. This will allow you to make adjustments and ensure that they are the right coping strategies for you.

This activity will help you cope with overwhelming emotions during your recovery journey. With these firmly in place, your emotions can be effectively managed and give you the clarity of mind needed to move on to the next step of your recovery— improving your relationship with food to ensure a sustainable recovery.

CHAPTER 7

HEALING YOUR RELATIONSHIP WITH FOOD— STRATEGIES FOR SUSTAINABLE RECOVERY

When you starve yourself, you feed your demons.

—ANONYMOUS

Working toward your recovery from BED requires a holistic approach. You have to address all aspects of the disorder, from the emotional to the physical. Included in the physical aspects is addressing your diet. However, it does not just involve what you should and should not eat. Addressing your diet during BED recovery entails healing your relationship with food. You have to change the way you think and feel about food. Most of all, you have to realize that food is not the sole cause of your BED—there are other factors involved.

However, when you improve your relationship with food, you ensure a sustainable recovery because you will not fall into the same traps again. In this chapter, we will cover strategies that you implement to improve your relationship with food and ensure positive results for your recovery.

Mindful Eating

One of the occurrences of BED that we discussed earlier is the fact that people binge on food without being aware of how much food they are eating. I distinctly remember the shock and horror I would experience when I realized how much food I had consumed during a binge eating session—it was closely followed by the immense shame and guilt that we all know too well.

As part of the recovery journey, one of the practices that is recommended to alleviate this is mindful eating. Mindful eating refers to bringing awareness to what you eat. This entails everything from preparation to taste to how your body feels when eating. There is no judgment associated with eating, no other criticism or negative thoughts—just how you are feeling while eating. It is an extremely useful practice, even for those who do not have a BED because our meals are often rushed and there is not enough focus on the actual feeding of our bodies.

Mindful eating allows you to:

- eat slowly and without distraction
- pay attention to signs of physical hunger
- recognize signs of emotional hunger
- eat until you are full and not beyond that point
- engage all your senses
- manage the guilt and anxiety you may have toward food
- notice the effects food has on your body
- notice the effects food has on your feelings
- gain a new appreciation of food and how it nourishes and satisfies your body

You can already tell from how mindful eating works that it will be an excellent tool to add to your BED recovery toolkit. It changes how you think about food, allowing you to let go of the shame of bingeing and embrace the wonders of how food nourishes our body, feeds our soul, and gives us the fuel we need to not just survive, but thrive.

Benefits of Mindful Eating

I have always believed that the one benefit of mindful eating is that it allows you to change your views about food. It's not about healthy food or junk foods, snacks or meals—it's just about how your senses come alive when you eat. If you simply bring your focus to that, your entire perspective of food changes and you are less likely to binge if you develop this habit. And that's only the beginning—there are several other benefits that arise because of this and are all linked to the act of mindful eating. Let's take a closer look at these.

Provides a Moment of Stillness in Our Busy Lives

We can often feel rushed when we are eating, which begs the question, "*What are we actually eating for?*" Are we eating to satisfy our hunger, to enjoy foods we like, or just because we have to? Sometimes, eating is not even done out of hunger but simply because it is time to eat as dictated by our schedule or planners. When we begin to eat mindfully, we learn to pause and take in the moment. We are conscious of our hunger, tastes, feelings, and satiation when we eat. We truly give ourselves a break—a moment of stillness that provides clarity and reinvigorates us to continue with the rest of our day.

Helps Identify When You Are Truly Hungry

When you practice mindful eating, you become more familiar with your eating habits overall. If you eat when you are not hungry, you will begin to easily notice it. Furthermore, you will become more adept at identifying when you are truly physically hungry.

Enjoy Your Food More

One of the fun benefits of mindful eating is that you will begin to enjoy your food more. You will start to really taste your food and notice things that you didn't before. You could even discover foods that you don't like the taste of as well. This will help you eliminate these items and have foods that you actually like the taste of.

Make Better Choices Regarding What You Eat

Mindful eating allows you to really pay attention to what you eat. You will be more observant of not only the taste but also the type of food you eat. It makes it easier to eliminate unhealthy foods or those that do not leave you feeling nourished or full. Mindful eating is not about dieting or counting calories but instead allows you to make decisions about food and how your body feels while you consume it and after.

You Stop Eating When Full

Just as you are able to identify when you are hungry, you will also be able to realize when you are full. Mindful eating causes you to eat slower and better gauge your body's level of fullness. Many of us eat well beyond the point of feeling full because our brain takes a while to catch up to the amount of food we eat when we eat quickly. By taking the time to be mindful while eating, our entire body is in sync and can register the moment you are full.

Appreciate Food More

When you are mindful when eating, you will find that you naturally become mindful when preparing your food and when buying your groceries. This gives you a greater appreciation of where your food comes from and what you eat. You will find yourself making different purchase decisions, and automatically eating healthier.

Let Go of Shame Associated With Eating

Mindful eating allows people with BED to let go of the shame associated with eating. Many of us feel ashamed when we eat, especially if it is after a binge eating episode. However, being mindful while eating gives you something else to focus on. You are paying attention to your body while eating and, in doing so, are being proactive in letting go of any shame.

Improves Digestion

When you practice mindful eating, you tend to eat slower as you evaluate the physical and mental aspects of eating. As a result, you can enjoy improved digestion because you are chewing your food properly, making it the optimal consistency to move through your digestive tract and be properly digested. Most of the time, we eat too quickly, causing our digestive systems to battle as they cannot keep up with what they need to do.

How to Practice Mindful Eating

To implement mindful eating during your meals, you have to focus your attention on your meal. Thus, you must put your phone away, stop eating at your desk while you work, and definitely switch the television off. All your awareness and senses must be focused on your food. It does take some time to get used to the process, but it gets easier the more you do it. Just remember to bring your attention back to your food when your mind starts to drift. Here are some helpful tips that can help you practice mindful eating.

Question Your Senses

Whether you are shopping, preparing, or eating, you should aim to employ all your senses when it comes to food. Question your senses as you partake in a meal.

Notice the smells, tastes, feels, looks, and sounds that arise while you eat. This will make you focus more intently on your meal and allow you to eat mindfully.

Spark Your Curiosity

Be curious about your food and how your body reacts to it. Observe your feelings, your physical state, and how you approach eating. Do you eat in a certain order, ensure you get a bit of everything on your plate with every bite, or leave your favorites for last? Everything from your posture to how you hold your cutlery should make you curious about yourself and your eating habits. It might even let you discover more about yourself; bringing a whole new level of self-awareness.

Evaluate Your Hunger

You should only be eating when you are hungry. Not when you are bored, not when you are starving because you missed lunch, and not because someone asked you to keep them company. We often eat for the wrong reasons instead of paying attention to our hunger. Therefore, paying attention to your body, and learning to differentiate hunger from thirst and boredom can be a great way to practice mindfulness in general.

Eat Slower

One of the most effective ways to practice mindful eating is to slow down when you are having a meal. Have you ever paid attention to how long it takes you to finish a meal? You may be surprised as to how fast it actually happens. If you slow down the process by first appreciating the look of your meal before eating and then putting your cutlery down between bites, you can then focus on chewing your food properly and slowing down your meal. This will not just aid digestion, but help you concentrate on your meal.

These tips are useful and while implementing them becomes easier over time, people will still have a bit of difficulty practicing them at every meal. For example, when sharing a meal with friends, conversations may distract you from your food. This is perfectly normal and you should not beat yourself up about it. However, you can still practice small parts of mindful eating like evaluating your hunger, thinking about the taste of your food, and eating until you are full. It takes time to get the balance right but if you are committed to your recovery journey, in time you will find your rhythm.

Tracking Chart

As you embrace mindful eating, consider integrating a "Tracking Chart" into your journal for a more comprehensive overview. On a fresh page, layout columns with these headings from left to right: **Date, Start Time, Pre-Eating Hunger Level, Pre-Eating Emotions, Food Consumed, Post-Eating Emotions, Post-Eating Hunger Level, End Time, Dining Context**, and **Overall Reflections.**

Date: Write down the date you are having your meal or snack.

Start Time: Note the time you start to eat your meal or snack.

Hunger Level (pre and post): Rate your hunger on a scale of 1-10, with 1 being very hungry and 10 being extremely full.

Emotions (pre and post): Describe how you feel or what you're thinking prior to eating (pre), and after consuming your meal or snack (post).

Food Consumed: List everything you eat and drink, whether it's a small snack or a full meal. Include portion sizes.

End Time: Note the time at the end of your meal or snack.

Dining Context: Specify whether you are dining with company or alone? Note your posture (standing or sitting) and your overall state (rushed or relaxed).

Overall Reflections: Summarize your thoughts and feelings about your eating experiences for the day.

Here are five essential guidelines to keep in mind while recording these entries in your Tracking Chart - or when later reviewing them to identify patterns, triggers, or areas of concern that you'd like to address:

1. **Consistency:** Strive to consistently record every meal and snack. A more comprehensive journal will provide better insights into your patterns and triggers.

2. **Honesty:** Be truthful with yourself when documenting your food intake and emotions. Your journal is a personal tool, so there's no need to exaggerate or downplay your experiences.

3. **Regular Reflection:** Periodically review your journal entries. Look for recurring patterns in your eating habits, emotional triggers, or situations that may lead to binge episodes.

4. **Practice Self-Compassion:** Remember that recovery from BED is a process, and there will be ups and downs. Use your journal as a tool for self-reflection and growth, rather than as a source of self-criticism.

5. **Set Realistic Goals:** Utilize the insights from your journal to establish realistic and achievable goals for gradually improving your eating habits and emotional coping strategies.

You are encouraged to adapt the column headings to align with your unique eating routine or tracking desires. Perhaps you may wish to add other headings such as "Triggers" or "Stressors" before/after. The data you will need to concentrate on most should be the areas you need to improve upon during meals.

Remember, this tool is designed to observe patterns rather than count calories or set boundaries in your eating journey.

Record all of your observations in your journal. For instance, did you eat too rapidly? Or, were you distracted while dining with others, leading to a hurried meal? Reflect on these insights and focus on making the necessary adjustments that will be best for you and your relationship with food.

Strategy #5: Nourishing Your Body—Balanced Nutrition, Meal Planning, Recipes, and Building a Healthy, Structured Eating Pattern

Balanced Nutrition

A balanced nutrition approach seeks to nourish the body and mind while fostering a healthy relationship with food. It's about listening to one's body cues and practicing mindful eating. Such a plan typically includes a variety of foods from all food groups, with an emphasis on whole grains, lean proteins, fruits, vegetables, and healthy fats. Portion control plays a crucial role, aiding you to become more attuned to your hunger and fullness signals. It's equally important to incorporate flexibility, allowing for occasional indulgences without guilt. Furthermore, as previously discussed, incorporating consistent meals and snacks into your daily routine can play a crucial role in stabilizing blood sugar levels and lowering the risk of experiencing binge episodes. In this holistic approach, nutrition is not just about the body; it's also about nourishing the soul and addressing the emotional aspects that often underlie binge eating behaviors. A balanced nutrition plan for individuals with BED promotes not only physical well-being but also psychological and emotional healing.

Meal Planning

The following serves as an illustrative example of a balanced meal plan for BED recovery. Keep in mind that your individual preferences may differ, and any dietary restrictions should be considered when crafting a personalized meal plan. It's highly advisable to consult with a healthcare professional or registered dietitian to create a tailored plan that aligns best with your needs.

This example meal plan emphasizes whole, unprocessed foods, balanced meals and snacks, and mindful eating practices to support BED recovery.

Breakfast:

- Protein Source (e.g., eggs, Greek yogurt, tofu)
- Whole grains (e.g., whole grain toast, oatmeal)
- A small serving of fruits or vegetables
- Healthy fat source (e.g., avocado, nuts, or seeds)
- A glass of water or herbal tea

Mid-Morning Snack:

- Protein-rich snack (e.g., cottage cheese, lean turkey, or a small handful of almonds)
- A piece of fruit (e.g., an apple or a banana), or vegetable
- A glass of water

Lunch:

- Lean protein source (e.g., grilled chicken breast, fish, or beans)
- Quinoa salad with mixed vegetables (e.g., bell peppers, cucumbers, and cherry tomatoes)

- Whole grains (e.g., quinoa, brown rice, or whole wheat pasta)
- A small serving of healthy fats (e.g., olive oil or avocado)
- A glass of water or herbal tea

Afternoon Snack:

- Carrot and celery stick with hummus
- A handful of unsalted mixed nuts
- A glass of water

Dinner:

- Lean protein source (similar to lunch, or Baked salmon, or a plant-based protein source (e.g., lentils or chickpeas)
- Steamed or roasted vegetables (e.g., broccoli and cauliflower)
- Whole grains or starchy vegetables (e.g., sweet potatoes, quinoa)
- A small serving of healthy fats
- A glass of water or herbal tea

Evening Snack (if needed):

- A small, balanced option like a handful of berries, or a slice of whole grain bread with peanut butter, or sliced cucumber or cherry tomatoes
- A glass of water

Mindful eating reminders:

Firstly, practice mindful eating during every meal and snack, taking the time to savor each bite and tune into your body's hunger and fullness cues. This mindful approach can help you foster a healthier relationship with food.

Secondly, make a conscious effort to focus on the nutritional value of the foods you select, aiming for a well-rounded mix of macronutrients, including protein, carbohydrates, and healthy fats. This balance supports your overall well-being.

Thirdly, maintain proper hydration throughout the day by regularly consuming water or soothing herbal teas. Staying hydrated is essential for overall health and can help prevent unnecessary food cravings.

Lastly, embrace flexibility in your meal plan, allowing for occasional treats or indulgences in moderation, while steering clear of highly processed foods, sugary snacks, and excessive caffeine. This balanced approach to eating encourages a more sustainable and enjoyable relationship with food.

Recipes

Below, are several examples of delicious and nutritious recipes that you may enjoy trying for a breakfast, lunch, or dinner:

Greek Yogurt Parfait:

Ingredients:

- 1 cup Greek yogurt
- 1 tablespoon honey or a pinch of cinnamon
- 1/2 cup fresh berries (strawberries, blueberries, raspberries)
- 2 tablespoons crushed almonds or walnuts

Instructions:

1. In a bowl or glass, spoon in the Greek yogurt.
2. Drizzle honey or sprinkle cinnamon on top for added flavor.

3. Add a layer of fresh berries.

4. Sprinkle crushed almonds or walnuts over the berries.

5. Enjoy your wholesome parfait!

Veggie Omelet:

Ingredients:

- 2 eggs, whisked
- 1/4 cup diced bell peppers
- 1/4 cup diced onions
- 1/4 cup chopped spinach
- 1/4 cup low-fat cheese
- Cooking spray or a touch of oil for the pan

Instructions:

1. Heat a non-stick skillet over medium heat and lightly coat it with cooking spray or a small amount of oil.
2. Add diced bell peppers, onions, and chopped spinach. Sauté for a few minutes until vegetables are tender.
3. Pour the whisked eggs evenly over the veggies.
4. Once the eggs are mostly set, sprinkle low-fat cheese on one half of the omelet.
5. Carefully fold the omelet in half.
6. Cook for another minute until the cheese is melted and the omelet is cooked through.
7. Serve with whole-grain toast.

Overnight Oats:

Ingredients:

- 1/2 cup rolled oats
- 1 cup almond milk (or your choice of milk)
- 1 tablespoon chia seeds
- 1 tablespoon maple syrup
- 1/2 banana, sliced
- Chopped nuts and a pinch of cinnamon for topping

Instructions:

1. In a jar, combine rolled oats, almond milk, chia seeds, and maple syrup.
2. Stir well to combine all ingredients.
3. Top with sliced banana, chopped nuts, and a pinch of cinnamon.
4. Seal the jar and refrigerate overnight.
5. In the morning, give it a quick stir and enjoy your nutritious breakfast!

Grilled Chicken and Avocado Sandwich (for two)

Ingredients:

- 2 boneless, skinless chicken breasts
- 1 tablespoon olive oil
- 1 teaspoon paprika
- 1/2 teaspoon dried oregano
- Salt and pepper to taste
- 4 slices of whole-grain bread
- 1 ripe avocado, sliced
- 1 cup mixed greens (e.g., spinach, arugula, or lettuce)
- 1 medium tomato, thinly sliced
- 1/4 red onion, thinly sliced
- Dijon mustard or hummus for spreading (optional)

Instructions:

1. In a small bowl, combine olive oil, paprika, dried oregano, salt, and pepper.
2. Brush the mixture over the chicken breasts to coat them evenly.
3. Preheat a grill or grill pan over medium-high heat.
4. Grill the chicken for about 6-8 minutes per side or until it's cooked through and has grill marks. The internal temperature should reach 165°F (74°C).
5. Remove the chicken from the grill and let it rest for a few minutes before slicing it into thin strips.
6. Lay out the four slices of whole-grain bread (toasted if preferred).
7. If desired, spread Dijon mustard or hummus on one side of each slice for added flavor.
8. On two of the slices, layer the grilled chicken strips, avocado slices, mixed greens, tomato slices, and red onion.
9. Top each sandwich with the remaining slices of bread.
10. Press down gently to compact the ingredients together.
11. Slice the Grilled Chicken and Avocado Sandwiches in half diagonally.
12. Serve and enjoy this balanced and delicious lunch with that special someone!

Quinoa Salad with Chickpeas:

Ingredients:

- 1 cup cooked quinoa
- 1/2 cup canned chickpeas, drained and rinsed
- 1/2 cup diced cucumber
- 1/2 cup cherry tomatoes, halved
- 2 tablespoons chopped fresh parsley
- Olive oil and lemon juice for dressing
- Salt and pepper to taste
- Leafy greens (e.g., spinach or arugula) for serving

Instructions:

1. In a large bowl, combine cooked quinoa, chickpeas, diced cucumber, cherry tomatoes, and fresh parsley.
2. Drizzle with olive oil and lemon juice for dressing. Season with salt and pepper to taste.
3. Toss everything together until well mixed.
4. Serve the salad on a bed of leafy greens for added freshness.

Vegetable and Lentil Soup:

Ingredients:

- 1 cup dried green or brown lentils, rinsed
- 2 carrots, diced
- 2 celery stalks, diced
- 1 onion, diced
- 2 cups chopped spinach
- 1 bay leaf
- 6 cups vegetable broth
- 1 teaspoon dried thyme
- 1 teaspoon dried rosemary
- Salt and pepper to taste

Instructions:

1. In a large pot, sauté the diced onion, carrots, and celery until they start to soften.
2. Add lentils, bay leaf, thyme, rosemary, and vegetable broth.
3. Bring to a boil, then reduce heat, cover, and simmer for about 25-30 minutes or until lentils are tender.
4. Stir in chopped spinach and cook for an additional 5 minutes.
5. Remove the bay leaf and season with salt and pepper.
6. Serve the soup with whole-grain crackers.

Turkey and Avocado Wrap:

Ingredients:

- 1 whole-grain wrap or tortilla
- 3-4 slices of lean turkey breast
- 1/4 avocado, sliced
- Lettuce leaves
- Tomato slices
- Optional: Greek yogurt or hummus for creaminess

Instructions:

1. Lay the whole-grain wrap on a clean surface.
2. Place the turkey slices evenly on the wrap.
3. Add sliced avocado, lettuce leaves, and tomato slices.
4. If desired, add a dollop of Greek yogurt or hummus for extra flavor.
5. Roll up the wrap, tucking in the sides as you go.
6. Cut it into bite-sized pieces and enjoy!

Grilled Salmon with Quinoa and Asparagus:

Ingredients:

- 2 salmon fillets
- 1 tablespoon olive oil
- 1 teaspoon lemon juice
- 1/2 teaspoon garlic powder
- 1/2 teaspoon dried dill (or fresh if available)
- Salt and pepper to taste
- 1 cup cooked quinoa
- Steamed asparagus spears

Instructions:

1. Preheat your grill or grill pan to medium-high heat.
2. In a small bowl, mix olive oil, lemon juice, garlic powder, dried dill, salt, and pepper to create a marinade.
3. Brush the salmon fillets with the marinade on both sides.
4. Grill the salmon for about 4-5 minutes per side or until it flakes easily with a fork.
5. While the salmon is grilling, prepare the quinoa according to package instructions.
6. Steam the asparagus until tender, usually 3-4 minutes.
7. Serve the grilled salmon on a bed of cooked quinoa with steamed asparagus on the side.

Stir-Fried Tofu and Veggies:

Ingredients:

- 1 block extra-firm tofu, cubed
- 2 cups mixed vegetables (e.g., broccoli florets, bell peppers, snap peas)
- 2 tablespoons low-sodium soy sauce
- 1 teaspoon grated ginger
- 2 cloves garlic, minced
- 1 tablespoon sesame oil
- Cooked brown rice

Instructions:

1. Press the tofu to remove excess moisture and cut it into cubes.
2. Heat sesame oil in a large skillet or wok over medium-high heat.
3. Add tofu cubes and stir-fry until they turn golden brown on all sides. Remove from the pan and set aside.
4. In the same pan, add a bit more sesame oil if needed, then add minced garlic and grated ginger. Stir-fry for about 30 seconds.

5. Add mixed vegetables and stir-fry for 3-4 minutes until they start to become tender.
6. Return the tofu to the pan and drizzle low-sodium soy sauce over everything. Stir-fry for another 2-3 minutes.
7. Serve over cooked brown rice.

Baked Chicken and Sweet Potato:

Ingredients:

- 2 boneless, skinless chicken breasts
- 2 medium sweet potatoes, peeled and sliced
- 1 cup Brussels sprouts, halved
- 2 tablespoons olive oil
- 1 teaspoon paprika
- 1/2 teaspoon dried thyme
- Salt and pepper to taste

Instructions:

1. Preheat your oven to 375°F (190°C).
2. In a bowl, mix olive oil, paprika, dried thyme, salt, and pepper to create a marinade.
3. Brush the chicken breasts and sweet potato slices with the marinade.
4. Place the chicken, sweet potatoes, and halved Brussels sprouts on a baking sheet.
5. Bake for about 25-30 minutes or until the chicken is cooked through, and the sweet potatoes are tender.
6. Serve and enjoy this well-balanced and delicious dinner!

Structured Eating

An important part of recovery is building a structured eating pattern. This is when you have an organized way in which you eat. At this point, I need to stress that structured eating is not a restrictive diet. You're not putting restrictions on your eating. Instead, you are creating a healthy, balanced pattern whereby you eat at the correct intervals. This ensures that you stay full throughout the day, have the proper nutrients and vitamins to fuel your daily activities, and can heal your relationship with food.

Essentially, an ideal structured eating pattern will include eating one hour after waking, meals set a maximum of four hours apart, with a total of three meals and not more than four healthy snacks daily. Structured eating also entails eating the correct proportion of food groups to ensure a healthy, nutritious, and balanced eating plan.

By implementing structured eating, there is no need for restrictive diets and you can effectively break your BED cycle. Furthermore, if you keep your body nourished by following structured eating patterns, you are less likely to experience cravings that could lead to a binge eating episode. By establishing structured eating patterns, individuals can actively progress in their BED recovery.

The Benefits of Structured Eating

Structured eating patterns can be beneficial to everyone but they are especially beneficial for those who are recovering from an eating disorder. Let's take a look at what structured eating can do for your recovery.

- Structured eating involves organization and meal planning. This leads to more mindful grocery shopping, food preparation, and eating. In turn, you will be less tempted to deviate from your list and buy foods that you would normally binge on.
- Due to the plan you develop, you end up creating healthy boundaries when it comes to your meals. The aim of structured eating is to be consistent

with balanced meals and not how much you eat. However, as you practice mindful eating alongside meal planning, you will automatically end up eating healthier and stop eating when you are physically full.

- Structured eating can easily fit into your daily routines and you don't have to worry about abandoning it for special events. There is no stress about what you're going to eat because your meal will fit into your plan.

- Planning your meals as part of implementing structured eating will also minimize the amount of time you have to think about food decisions and shopping, which are two areas that people with BED may find difficult.

- Structured eating can also help fix your metabolism. Restrictive diets and skipping meals will slow down your metabolism significantly as your body tries to conserve energy. By eating regular meals and being consistent, you can speed up your metabolism once again.

Tips for Implementing Structured Eating

Structured eating is one of the first steps a professional might recommend to help you recover from BED. However, food can be a difficult subject to navigate at the start of your BED recovery. This is why it is crucial to have patience and implement each aspect strategically to strengthen your approach to recovery. It is only through working through the cause of your BED, your emotional triggers, and adjusting your mindset that you can firmly heal your relationship with food. Here are some useful tips that will help you implement structured eating.

- Take some time on a Sunday to plan your meals for the week ahead. Choose seven breakfasts, seven lunches, and seven dinners—don't forget about your snacks, either! Whether you want them on certain days or allow yourself to switch them around is up to you. The main aim is to have a plan so you don't have to focus on it during the week.

- Remember that structured eating does not mean you have to stick to a boring diet. Ensure variation in your meals and that they include foods you genuinely like.

- When you have this weekly meal plan, create your shopping list. This gives you a list to stick to and won't leave you nervous while you are at the store.

- Share your journey with your family and friends so that they are aware of your intentions. This will make the entire process easier and you won't feel awkward when they question your eating habits.

- Writing in your journal through this process might help you identify what does and does not work for you in your structured eating plan. For example, if you find yourself feeling hungry after a particular meal, you may have to adjust your portion size or consider the contents of the meal. Remember, you can use your Tracking Chart to track the start and end times of your meals to gauge if you need to slow down while eating.

Structured eating provides you with a plan that will help minimize food disruptions that are common with eating disorders. You won't be restricting yourself, risking cravings, or constantly feeling ashamed for thinking about food. There will be a plan in place that ensures that your body gets what it needs and you don't have the emotional burden that you have come to associate with food. Over time, this will help you change how you perceive food and enable a sustainable recovery from BED.

Managing Food Cravings—Coping with Triggers

When it comes to food, one of the major hurdles to overcome once you begin to follow an eating plan is food cravings. We all have food cravings, but when it comes to BED, food cravings can easily trigger a binge eating episode. This is why it is crucial to learn how to manage these as part of your BED recovery. Cravings don't just appear for no reason. They have a definite cause and figuring out what the cause—or causes—of your cravings will help you manage them better.

The main causes of cravings are

- **Emotional Eating:** This is one of the main causes of cravings for people with BED. Cravings are triggered when we want to avoid our emotions.
- **Self-Sabotage:** Sometimes, when you are well into your recovery and things are going smoothly, you may be tempted by cravings that are known trigger foods for your BED. It is a form of self-sabotage that makes us crave even more food when we try to compensate for going off-course.
- **Hormones:** For women, changes in hormones caused by menstruation, pregnancy, and menopause, or hormonal imbalances caused by disorders can cause cravings.
- **Food Imbalance:** Have you ever craved candy after eating a bag of chips? And then after you have some candy, you want something salty again? These cravings are caused by eating too much of one type of food. Your body seeks balance and then craves something on the opposite end of the spectrum. Eating a more balanced diet that avoids extremes can help you manage these cravings.
- **Lack of Nutrients:** When our bodies lack the vital nutrients needed for proper function, it will result in cravings. However, the cravings are not specific to the lack of nutrients and you may eat foods with low nutritional value. As a result, you will have constant cravings until you address the true cause.
- **Thirst:** Many people confuse thirst with hunger. As such, you may crave a snack but what you actually need is water. This is why one of the easiest ways to alleviate cravings is to drink some water to ensure that you are just not thirsty.

- **Seasonal:** Yes, whether you are aware of it or not, it is possible to get seasonal cravings. You might crave pumpkin spice lattes in fall, warm, hearty soups in winter, or even fresh watermelon in summer. This is all because your brain connects the season to these foods and causes cravings.

- **Nostalgia:** Sometimes we crave things from our childhood out of comfort. For example, when we are sick, we might crave foods that our mom made for us, or maybe when we celebrate an accomplishment, we need a slice of cake because that's what our parents gave us as a reward when we were little. They're small things, but unless you pay attention to them, you won't realize that it is the source of your cravings.

- **Boredom:** When we feel bored with our jobs or don't have any stimulating activities in our lives, we may get food cravings to inject some excitement into our lives. We use food as a way to compensate for the lack of challenge or even the lack of company in our daily lives.

It is not uncommon for more than one cause of food cravings to be present in our lives. However, that doesn't mean that you have to fear them messing up your recovery process. You have to accept that these cravings exist for a reason and to alleviate them, you have to address the cause and not give in to them.

Here's what you can do to manage food cravings effectively:

- Drink water as your first line of defense. You could just be thirsty and this is the easiest way to curb food cravings.

- Planning and eating healthy, balanced meals will address nutritional food cravings and significantly decrease cravings throughout the day.

- Avoid restrictive diets that will amplify food cravings.

- Be mindful of your emotions and your moods. Evaluate if they are driving your food cravings.

- Find activities that stimulate your mind and alleviate boredom.

- Understand that food cravings occur due to nostalgia and seasons. Have a plan in place to avoid overindulgence during these times. You can substitute healthier snack options that satisfy these cravings.

- Separate a binge from a craving in your mind. Accepting that a food craving has a cause and must not result in a binge eating episode is crucial for your recovery.

- If a binge eating episode is triggered by a food craving, document it in your journal to learn from the experience and identify trigger foods for your BED.

Food cravings don't have to mean the end of your BED recovery process. Understanding where they come from and what you need to do to avoid them is important. Following a structured eating pattern, staying hydrated, and being mindful will greatly help you avoid food cravings.

Workbook Activity: Designing a Personalized Meal Plan

This workbook activity will help you design a personalized meal plan that supports your recovery by considering both your emotional and physical well-being. If you give each of these steps careful consideration, you arm yourself with a powerful tool that will help you overcome BED. For some of these next steps, it may be helpful to do some research on-line to help determine all the different foods in the food groups as well as portion sizes and nutritional values. So, grab your notebook or write directly in the space provided below.

Step 1: Assess Your Nutritional Needs

The first step to creating a personalized meal plan is to assess your nutritional needs. This means that you need to consider any existing health concerns such as high cholesterol or blood pressure. In doing so, you will have an idea of what foods you can include in your plan.

_____

_____

_____

Step 2: Define Your Meal Structure

A typical meal structure should consist of three well balanced, healthy meals and three healthy snacks each day. However, you need to figure out if this works for you, your lifestyle, and your nutritional needs. Maybe you prefer eating six small meals throughout the day and snacking is something you want to avoid as it is a trigger for your BED. You will know what works best for you to ensure sustained energy to fuel your activities throughout the day.

_____

_____

_____

Step 3: Choose Balanced Food Groups

When putting together your meal plan, you need to aim for a balanced combination of food groups. This includes whole grains, lean proteins, healthy fats, fruits, vegetables, and dairy (or dairy alternatives if you prefer). Select foods that you enjoy and that will provide the nutrients your body needs.

_____

_____

_____

Step 4: Portion Sizes and Serving Guidelines

Each food group will have appropriate portion sizes. You can check these online or work with a dietician to ensure that your meals leave you feeling full and support your health goals.

_____

_____

_____

Step 5: Meal Prep and Planning

Meal prep and planning are an essential part of your overall meal plan for recovery. It will help you plan your meals so that they fit into your schedule and lifestyle. For example, if you know you don't have enough time during the week to cook, you can implement batch cooking on the weekends which will make your life easy during the week. Furthermore, with a clear plan for the week ahead, you don't have to think about what you want to eat or feel like eating every single day.

_____

_____

_____

Step 6: Reflective Questions

The following questions will help you gain further insights into your personalized meal plan.

- Do you have any favorite nutritious food that you can include in your meal plan?

_____

_____

- How can you incorporate more variety and color into your meals?

_____

_____

- Have you identified any trigger foods or ingredients that you need to keep in mind when planning your meals?

_____

_____

- How can you ensure that your meal plan meets your daily nutrient and energy requirements?

_____

_____

- Can you think of any strategies that will help you sustain the act of meal planning and prepping?

_____

_____

- How will your meal plan support your physical and emotional well-being in your BED recovery journey?

_____

_____

- Do you have any specific goals associated with your meal plan? What are they?

_____

_____

- How will you implement accountability for your personalized meal plan?

_____

_____

- What strategies can you use to navigate challenges or setbacks that may arise while sticking to your meal plan?

_____

_____

- How can you practice self-compassion and adaptability if your meal plan needs adjustments?

_____

_____

Remember, this personalized meal plan is a guide that will help you in your BED recovery. However, it is never set in stone. A meal plan must be flexible and evolve with you as your needs and preferences change over time. Therefore, it is necessary to regularly assess your meal plan to check if it needs to be modified. If you are unsure of anything or feel overwhelmed by the number of options to consider, you can always consult a professional to get the guidance you need.

Healing your relationship with food is a personal journey, and for any relationship to work you have to be committed to it. It will take time and there will be a fair amount of trial and error. However, with the right mindset and your goals clearly in your view, you can reach your final destination after following your path to BED recovery. In the next chapter, we will cover the last three strategies that can sustain your recovery and ensure long-term success.

CHAPTER 8

THRIVING BEYOND BINGE EATING DISORDER

Make peace with the mirror and watch your reflection change.

—ANONYMOUS

Your path to BED recovery has been chartered throughout this book with helpful strategies that you can implement along the way. These strategies will help you navigate the journey, strengthening your approach and ensuring that you know how to approach setbacks and prevent relapses. In this chapter, I want to cover what happens next. So many self-help books I have come across will provide steps for a successful recovery. However, many miss a crucial point—what do you do after you recover? For your BED recovery to be sustainable, you need to know what to do after you are successful in overcoming BED. A successful journey is indeed the hard part, but sustaining your recovery is equally important. Let's get started on the three strategies that will ensure a sustainable, long-term recovery.

Strategy #6: Prioritizing Self-Care

We have briefly covered the importance of self-care previously when discussing the treatment options for BED. While it is indeed important to practice self-care during your recovery, it is also necessary for sustaining it. Your recovery journey is also a journey of self-discovery and when you finally come out on the other side, you have to ensure that you take care of your new sense of self. When you work so hard to heal your mind, body, and spirit, you must ensure that you nurture this new relationship with yourself.

The Four Pillars of Self-Care

Practicing self-care is one of the best ways to maintain your recovery from BED. It not only empowers you by learning how to deal with negative thoughts and emotions, but also teaches you how to evaluate your needs and nurture yourself from a holistic point of view. It gives you what you need to grow and reach your true potential by knowing who you are and what you value in life.

Self-care consists of four main components known as the four pillars of self-care. These are physical, emotional, mental, and spiritual self-care. By finding ways to implement these aspects of self-care into your daily life, you can free yourself from the chains of BED and forget the lies that led you astray from who you are.

Physical Self-Care

The physical aspect of self-care refers to taking care of the physical needs of our bodies. This is important for those recovering from BED as this form of self-care enables us to fulfill our nutritional needs. We can take care of our physical bodies by ensuring that we eat healthily and ensure that movement is a part of our day.

However, equally important is finding methods of relaxation, remembering to schedule our doctor's appointments, and paying attention to our body's needs.

People with eating disorders may look put together, but it is often just an act. They do not take care of themselves because they begin to believe that it is not important due to their negative self-image. As part of the recovery process, you will work to heal your relationship with your body and start treating it with the love and care it deserves. You need to sustain this practice beyond your recovery to ensure that you never forget how precious this relationship truly is.

Some great ways of practicing physical self-care long-term include:

- Nourishing your body inside and out by ensuring that you get the nutrients, vitamins, and minerals you need.
- Make time for personal grooming. When you look good, you feel good, and when you feel good, your self-confidence can truly shine. You worked hard for your recovery; you have every right to feel confident!
- Find ways to exercise daily. If you're not a fan of the gym, take your dog for a walk, play outdoors with your kids, or even take the stairs instead of the elevator. Any movement is better than none!
- Don't forget to rest. Our bodies need to rest to recuperate from the stress and tiredness that we experience. Getting enough sleep, treating yourself to a spa day, and taking time to be by yourself are important self-care practices. If you know what your body needs to feel refreshed and invigorated, it will help you be more productive in the future.
- As part of your BED recovery, you would have learned about meal plans and structured eating. Ensure that your food meets your physical requirements and keeps you satiated and healthy.

Emotional Self-Care

To practice emotional self-care is to accept your emotions for what they are and allow them to run their course without affecting your mental and physical health. To do so, you have to work on ways to identify your emotions and recognize how they affect your thoughts and behaviors. When you learn more about your emotions, you can begin to understand yourself and your actions better. In turn, you will stop reacting to your emotions and instead make sound, conscious decisions about your actions.

Emotional self-care practices include

- journaling
- meditation
- creative pursuits such as art, music, or dance
- self-reflection
- spending time with friends and family
- mindfulness
- practicing gratitude

Mental Self-Care

Mental self-care is a natural addition to your BED recovery and should be continued indefinitely to sustain it. You have to take care of your mental health to ensure your overall health and well-being. Nurturing your mind is just as important as nurturing your body.

As such, you should take time to practice mental self-care as part of your self-care routines. This will include practicing mindfulness to be aware of your thoughts. The more mindful you are, the easier it becomes to recognize distorted thought patterns, negative relationships, and situations that interfere with your mental well-being. Another great way to take care of your mental health is to continue learning. Trying new things and expanding your knowledge base encourages a growth mindset, which is great for personal growth.

Other examples of mental self-care include:

- Talking to your support group or therapist.
- Continuously learning through trying new hobbies, expanding your skillset to further your career, or learning new languages.
- Taking a break from social media or the internet in general. A break from your digital devices can help clear your mind and allow you to alleviate the stress and anxiety that online sources contribute to our lives.
- Spending time alone to self-reflect, re-center, and prioritize is just as important as spending time with others.

Spiritual Self-Care

Engaging in spiritual self-care is essential for nurturing one's mind and soul. While many find solace in meditation, crystals, nature, or praying to angels, my personal experience has led me to find true rest through a relationship with my Lord Jesus Christ. By dedicating time to daily prayer, scripture study, and reflection on Jesus' teachings, you allow yourself to be guided by His divine wisdom.

Trusting in God's plan, especially during moments of uncertainty or challenge, provides solace and guidance. Through Jesus, we are graced with unconditional love. Committing to spiritual practices centered around God is not just a ritual; it's an investment in your spiritual growth and well-being.

When you align your life with His purpose and love, you embrace a unique peace and clarity. Remember, you are His creation, and His love for you is boundless.

These four pillars of self-care provide a holistic approach to BED recovery. It addresses the physical, mental, and emotional aspects of treatment and allows people to get a deeper understanding of themselves. It can be a powerful tool in maintaining one's recovery and preventing relapses in the future. In addition, should relapses occur, they prevent a BED cycle from beginning again by teaching a person to be kind to themselves and keep moving forward.

Strategy #7: Body Acceptance and Self-Love—Embracing Your Unique Beauty

Body image can be incredibly difficult to talk about. Most people have a somewhat distorted and subjective image of their bodies—but most BED sufferers have a negative body image. In fact, when it comes to BED treatment, body image can be one of the hardest things to rectify and is usually one of the last symptoms of the disorder to treat (Muhlheim, 2023). This is because our body image is so deeply ingrained in our minds and has developed as a result of a lifetime of beliefs, thoughts, opinions, and behaviors.

Changing this takes time, but it is not impossible. Understanding that how you look has nothing to do with your value, and that you need to be as objective as possible when considering your body image, is crucial for your recovery. Furthermore, shedding the negative image you have of yourself can be an incredibly liberating process, allowing you to live your life without being held back by subjective and distorted thoughts.

The Four Aspects of Body Image

There are four aspects of body image that we need to work on to develop a positive image of our bodies.

- **Perceptual Body Image:** This is the way you see your body and is usually never accurate.
- **Cognitive Body Image:** The way you think about your body is considered your cognitive body image. Excessive thinking or worrying about your body image can affect your behavior leading to diets, eating disorders, and mental health issues.
- **Affective Body Image:** This refers to how you feel about your body.
- **Behavioral Body Image:** The way you behave due to your body image is included in this aspect of body image. If you have a negative body image, you tend to engage in behaviors that hinder your progress because you believe you are not worth it.

Having a positive body image means that we accept that our bodies may have limitations and that it is different from others, but we appreciate that they serve us, and we respect the truly amazing vessels that they are. We are all unique in so many ways—our bodies being one of them. The sooner we learn to accept this fact, the sooner we can get rid of the hold that BED has on many of us.

How to Change Your Body Image

To change your body image and solidify your recovery, you need to work on the way you see, feel, think, and behave toward your body. It is not an easy process because you have to break a lifetime of thoughts and behaviors. However, the key to developing a positive body image is to consistently work at it. You can't just stop when you think you are where you are supposed to be. It is a lifelong commitment and one that will not just sustain your BED recovery but also improve your relationship with yourself.

To improve your body image, you must:

- **Focus on the Positive:** Think about your skills and talents and how they have nothing to do with your body image. Your body image does not determine your value nor will it ever.
- **Don't Get Caught up in Negative Self-Talk:** If you find yourself picking on your body, or having negative thoughts about how you look, stop them immediately. Reframe them to show appreciation for your body and how it serves you every day.
- **Don't Compare Your Body to Others:** Everyone is different and unique—can you imagine how boring it would be if we all looked the same? Accept that differences are what make us beautiful and let go of any form of comparison.
- **Take a Break from Social Media:** If you find yourself experiencing negative thoughts or emotions about yourself and your body while scrolling through social media, consider taking a break from it. If that does not work, you can also stop following the accounts where you find this happening the most. Follow accounts that inspire positive thoughts and emotions instead.
- **Be Grateful:** Practice gratitude for your body and all that it allows you to do.

These are actions that you need to practice daily. Don't avoid your reflection in the mirror. In fact, you should use the mirror to practice the points mentioned above. The more comfortable you get with looking at yourself in the mirror, the more comfortable you become in your body. Challenge negative thoughts as soon as they arise and remember that your body is so much more than a shape, size, or weight.

Strategy #8: Practicing Positive Affirmations

The last strategy that you need to practice both during and after your BED recovery is positive self-talk or affirmations. The interest in positive affirmations has grown immensely in the last few years, but its efficacy can't be ignored. They really do work well. Although they are not some magical practices that produces immediate effects—it is only through constant repetition that you begin to see the positive effects of the practice. Positive affirmations can challenge negative thoughts; proving them untrue and giving you something positive to believe in. They can motivate you, inspire you, and boost your self-esteem. These are important aspects for maintaining your BED recovery and ensuring that your self-image remains positive long after.

Positive affirmations may seem weird at first. After all, they usually entail talking to yourself in front of the mirror and those with a negative self-image may find this extremely difficult or awkward to begin with. However, this act is intentional because it helps challenge negative thoughts head-on. As soon as negative self-talk or thoughts begin, you have an opportunity to squash them and gain confidence as you do.

Benefits of Positive Affirmations

Practicing positive self-talk can transform your life in numerous ways. Here are the main benefits of daily positive affirmations that can impact the lives of those recovering from BED.

Positive affirmations can

- decrease stress
- help us make positive changes in our lives by providing the right intentions

- improve academic performance

- prevent dwelling on negative thoughts by replacing them with positive ones

- help us identify areas we need to work on

- help you remain focused on your goals and motivate you to achieve them

- improve your mental health

- improve your physical health

- reduce anxiety

- encourage optimism

- boost self-esteem

- improve emotional regulation and self-control

Therefore, positive affirmations can help you maintain your recovery, ensure that you build confidence, and that you remain focused on your goals. They work very similarly to how CBT practices influence your thoughts, behaviors, and actions. However, in the case of positive affirmations, you say them out loud and not just think it.

How to Implement Positive Affirmations Daily

To implement positive affirmations daily, you have to choose your words carefully. These are the sayings that will challenge your negative thoughts and give you the motivation to work toward your goals. Therefore, you must put some thought into them. Don't just use affirmations you find on the internet, either. You can use them to get an idea of how they should be structured, but personalize them so that they connect with you on a personal level.

To create your own positive affirmations, you should aim to:

- **Always Use the Present Tense**: Don't use words like "will" or "should." Instead, use words such as "I am" or "I do."

- **Keep it Simple:** This means short sentences that are easy to remember and don't involve complicated vocabulary.

- **Be Realistic:** No one knows you better than yourself and this gives you the best opportunity to ensure that your affirmation matches your lifestyle and intentions.

- **Write Them Down:** Writing your affirmations on paper and placing them on your bedside table will act as a reminder because you will see them in the morning when you wake up and, in the evening, before you go to bed. Some people prefer to stick them on the bathroom mirror, while others even like to place them on the refrigerator door. It all depends on where you will see them.

- **Say Them Out Loud:** Say your affirmations out loud at least twice a day for five minutes. You need to say them with conviction and believe them.

- **Stay Consistent:** Consistency is key to this practice and doing them at the same time every day can help to make this a positive habit.

- **Use Apps to Remind Yourself:** There are mobile apps available that will help you with reminders and keeping records of your affirmations each day.

- **Keep it Fresh:** If you find yourself getting tired of saying the same things over and over each day, switch them up. You can introduce variation in your affirmations to keep things fresh.

Practicing positive affirmations is an excellent way to boost self-esteem, improve body image, and remind you of what is important after your BED recovery. However, they do take time and they might not work for everyone. If you find you are one of those people, you need to take some time and reflect on your affirmations. Is there something that is blocking you from believing them? Do you have some unprocessed trauma, emotions, or negative self-talk that is holding you back? You have to carefully evaluate your answers to these questions to get to the cause of the block.

Some examples of positive affirmations you can use as inspiration for writing your own include:

- I love the person I am becoming.
- I am grateful for the job I have.
- I am worthy of love.
- I am proud of myself.
- I can and I will.
- I believe in myself.
- I am resilient.
- I am strong and healthy.
- I avoid temptation.
- My health and happiness are my priorities.
- I am confident.
- I am getting better every day.
- I accept myself, my body, and my mind completely.
- I believe in myself.
- I am happy with who I am.
- I am not that person anymore.
- Obstacles are stepping stones.

Remember, you can personalize these statements and use them to declare your current intentions for your life. If you are consistent and believe in them, you are giving yourself a powerful motivator each and every day.

Workbook Activity: Creating a Daily Self-Care Routine

The final workbook activity we will cover is creating a daily self-care routine. This routine is integral to your BED recovery and in sustaining it thereafter. By creating

ALLEN CROSS

a daily routine, you ensure that you build healthy habits, implement self-care daily, and give yourself the tools you need to sustain your recovery long-term.

The steps below will guide you in this process.

Step 1: Reflect on Your Needs and Priorities

Take some time to sit and reflect on your priorities and requirements in life. You can separate these into different categories that reflect the four pillars of self-care—physical, emotional, mental, and spiritual well-being.

_____

_____

_____

Step 2: Identify Self-Care Activities

Find self-care activities that resonate with you. These would be activities that bring you joy, peace, and relaxation. You also need to ensure that they are realistic and can fit into your schedule. It is necessary to make time for self-care activities but they should not interfere with your daily activities.

_____

_____

_____

Step 3: Create a Daily Schedule

Now it's time to slot these self-care activities into your planner to create a daily schedule. You can use a physical or digital planner according to your preference. The main aim of creating a daily schedule is consistency. Although you don't have to do all the same activities at the same time every day, you want to ensure that it becomes evident that a specific time is dedicated to them.

_____

_____

_____

_____

Step 4: Reflective Questions

The following questions will help guide you in creating your self-care routine.

- Can you identify specific activities that make you feel nourished and cared for?

_____

_____

_____

_____

- Can you think of self-care activities that align with your values and interests?

_____

_____

_____

- Are there any self-care activities that you used to enjoy before but stopped due to lack of time or care? Do you want to re-implement these into your routine?

_____

_____

_____

- Which activities help you manage your emotions effectively?

_____

_____

_____

- Which activities help you manage your stress levels?

_____

_____

_____

- Are there ways in which you can prioritize self-care daily? What are they?

_____

_____

_____

- What time of day do you think would be best to implement self-care? Think about when you feel most energized and when you feel most tired. Which do you think would be better?

_____

_____

_____

- Can you identify any challenges that may arise in your self-care routine? How can you work to overcome them?

_____

_____

_____

_____

- Think about days when you are extremely busy. How can you adapt your routine to still ensure that you incorporate self-care?

_____

_____

_____

_____

- How will you ensure that you will stick to your self-care routine?

_____

_____

_____

_____

Step 5: Implement and Adjust

The final step is to start following your new self-care routine and observing how well it works. Chances are you won't get it right the first time but that's perfectly normal. You will need to refine your routine as you go to ensure that it is optimized for your needs and your daily schedule. Self-care is a continuous process and your routine will evolve over time as you do. Requirements will change, priorities will shift, and your schedule will undoubtedly change. However, committing yourself to self-care means that you will change your self-care routine accordingly each and every time.

Your well-being is the aim of BED recovery. Ensuring that you pursue self-care, a positive body image, and positive self-talk will strengthen every aspect of your life. It will give you the confidence necessary to leave BED in the past and take all the lessons you have learned into your future.

What happens next?

As you reach the conclusion of this workbook, it's important to remember that recovery from binge eating disorder is a journey, and as I have emphasized throughout this book, it's perfectly normal to have ups and downs along the way. You have, however, taken a significant step towards healing and gaining control over your relationship with food, but the journey doesn't end here.

If you're asking yourself, "So, what happens next?" the answer lies in your hands. You can choose to go back to the beginning of this workbook and work through it again, reinforcing the strategies and insights you've gained. Alternatively, you can revisit specific chapters, strategies, or activities that you feel need more attention. Remember, recovery is a personal process, and it's about finding what works best for you.

Be patient with yourself, celebrate your victories, and don't be discouraged by setbacks. Recovery is not a linear path, but with persistence and self-compassion, you can continue making progress toward a healthier and more fulfilling life. Keep moving forward, and remember that you have the strength within you to overcome binge eating disorder.

YOUR REVIEW CAN LIGHT THE WAY!

Hello, dear friend,

You're almost there, at the brink of completing 'A Roadmap to Recovery: Overcoming Binge Eating Disorder.' It's been an incredible journey, full of insights and growth. Before you dive into the conclusion and ponder the full scope of what you've learned, take a moment to reflect on the path you've walked.

Your insights and experiences have become a well of wisdom, invaluable to those just starting on their path to recovery. The strategies and lessons that have resonated with you have the power to guide and inspire others. By sharing your review, you're extending a hand to those still looking for their way.

Think of your review as a beacon of hope, a light guiding others through their darkest moments. When you share your story, the insights you've gained from these pages transform into a lifeline for someone else. It's a validation that their journey towards healing is possible and worthwhile. Let's ensure every word helps illuminate the path to health and understanding.

To leave your unique imprint, simply go to the link *https://www.Amazon. com/review/create-review?&asin=B0D32BJDMF*, or scan the QR code provided

Here, please click on the stars rating, then in "Add a written review", just pour your heart out. Your honest reflection is what matters most—your real, unembellished journey.

Your words can create ripples of change, touching hearts and offering strength to those in need. Your review is more than feedback; it's a gesture of empathy, a shared experience, a message that says, "You're not alone." It helps build a community of understanding, showing others that their journey is recognized and supported.

Moreover, the act of sharing your journey can be a source of joy, reinforcing your own progress and contributing to others' healing. Your review is a symbol of solidarity, an integral part of the recovery narrative, not only for you but for countless others.

So, as you approach the end of this book, please pause to leave your review. Your words are powerful and deeply valued, so thank you for sharing your voice, your experiences, and being a guiding light in someone else's recovery journey.

Your empathy. Your impact. Our shared path to recovery.

CONCLUSION

Recovery from a binge eating disorder is not impossible. It may feel like it if you have tried and failed before, but it just means that you have not discovered the right approach. This workbook has given you eight strategies and provided activities that help you determine how you should approach your BED recovery. Working through these on your own or with the guidance of a professional will give you a personalized plan for your recovery and how to sustain it. It will take time and you have to be patient with yourself as you navigate this journey. However, commitment and understanding are what will allow you to reach your destination. When you understand the reasons behind your BED and why your previous recovery attempts have not worked, you will have the information you need to move forward confidently.

Ensuring that you have the right mindset and learn from past failures is integral to this process. I know this because I have been in this situation before. Addressing the root cause of my disorder and developing healthy coping mechanisms to deal with it led me to overcome BED. You can't try to get rid of binge eating by only focusing on your diet because most of the time the eating is not the problem. Restrictive diets will only lead you to a faster relapse—you have to take a holistic approach that addresses the physical, mental, and emotional aspects of your disorder. This will give you the boost you need in the recovery process.

Most importantly, you have to improve your relationship with yourself. Forgive yourself and let go of the burdens of your past. You have everything you need for your recovery within you—you just have to tap into it and allow it to step out of the darkness it has been kept in. You must not blame yourself for setbacks, they are merely stepping stones to success. You will learn from every relapse and come back stronger with new tools to repair the potholes in the road you're on.

Believe in yourself and trust in your support system for added strength when you need it the most. Every small step forward you take is progress and you should be proud of it. Don't forget to celebrate your achievements because this will provide the motivation needed to continue. Buying this workbook was the first step—now you must be consistent, take action, and continue down the road to recovery that you've embarked upon. Never stop traveling down that road because your success is not only possible, it is inevitable -and I can't wait to hear all about it!

You can do this!

REFERENCES

Algorani, E. B., & Gupta, V. (2022, April 28). *Coping Mechanisms*. PubMed; StatPearls Publishing. https://www.ncbi.nlm.nih.gov/books/NBK559031/

Bakalar, J. L., Shank, L. M., Vannucci, A., Radin, R. M., & Tanofsky-Kraff, M. (2015). Recent Advances in Developmental and Risk Factor Research on Eating Disorders. *Current Psychiatry Reports, 17*(6). https://doi.org/10.1007/s11920-015-0585-x

Balzora, S. M. (2022, November 21). *Advice | Ask a Doctor: If I eat too much, will my stomach explode?* Washington Post. https://www.washingtonpost.com/wellness/2022/11/21/binge-eating-overeating-stomach-rupture/

Bogusz, K., Kopera, M., Jakubczyk, A., Trucco, E. M., Kucharska, K., Walenda, A., & Wojnar, M. (2020). Prevalence of alcohol use disorder among individuals who binge eat: a systematic review and meta-analysis. *Addiction, 116*(1), 18–31. https://doi.org/10.1111/add.15155

Bohon, C. (2019). Binge Eating Disorder in Children and Adolescents. *Child and Adolescent Psychiatric Clinics of North America, 28*(4), 549–555. https://doi.org/10.1016/j.chc.2019.05.003

Bothwell, S. (2022, March 10). *Vyvanse for Binge Eating Disorder*. Eating Disorder Hope. https://www.eatingdisorderhope.com/treatment-for-eating-disorders/medications/vyvanse

Craigen, K. (2017, November 22). *Four Common Misconceptions about Binge Eating Disorder*. Eating Disorder Hope. https://www.eatingdisorderhope.com/blog/4-misconceptions-bed

Davis, R. (2023, February 25). *How Restrictive Diets Mess with Our Brains and Lead to Bingeing.* Tiny Buddha. https://tinybuddha.com/blog/how-restrictive-diets-mess-with-our-brains-and-lead-to-bingeing/

Dweck, C. S. (2006). *Mindset: The New Psychology of Success.* Random House.

Ekern, B. (2021, February 25). *Long Term & Short Term Consequences of Binge Eating Disorder.* Eating Disorder Hope. https://www.eatingdisorderhope.com/blog/long-term-short-term-consequences-of-binge-eating-disorder

Erskine, H. E., & Whiteford, H. A. (2018). Epidemiology of binge eating disorder. *Current Opinion in Psychiatry, 31*(6), 462–470. https://doi.org/10.1097/yco.0000000000000449

Gill, S. K., & Kaplan, A. S. (2020). A retrospective chart review study of symptom onset, diagnosis, comorbidities, and treatment in patients with binge eating disorder in Canadian clinical practice. *Eating and Weight Disorders - Studies on Anorexia, Bulimia and Obesity, 26*(4). https://doi.org/10.1007/s40519-020-01026-y

Gluck, S. (2013). *Quotes on Eating Disorders.* HealthyPlace. https://www.healthyplace.com/insight/quotes/quotes-on-eating-disorders

Halse Anderson, L. (2009). *Wintergirls.* Viking Books for Young Readers.

Heal, D. J., & Smith, S. L. (2021). Prospects for new drugs to treat binge-eating disorder: Insights from psychopathology and neuropharmacology. *Journal of Psychopharmacology, 36*(6), 026988112110324. https://doi.org/10.1177/02698811211032475

Hudson, J. I., Hiripi, E., Pope, H. G., & Kessler, R. C. (2007). The Prevalence and Correlates of Eating Disorders in the National Comorbidity Survey Replication. *Biological Psychiatry, 61*(3), 348–358. https://doi.org/10.1016/j.biopsych.2006.03.040

Jenna. (2022, April 27). *What Is Self-Care & Why Is It Important in Eating Disorder Recovery?* The Renfrew Center. https://renfrewcenter.com/what-is-self-care-why-is-it-important-in-eating-disorder-recovery/

Kelly, A. C., & Carter, J. C. (2014). Self-compassion training for binge eating disorder: A pilot randomized controlled trial. *Psychology and Psychotherapy: Theory, Research and Practice, 88*(3), 285–303. https://doi.org/10.1111/papt.12044

Keski-Rahkonen, A. (2021). Epidemiology of binge eating disorder: prevalence, course, comorbidity, and risk factors. *Current Opinion in Psychiatry, 34*(6), 525–531. https://doi.org/10.1097/yco.0000000000000750

Kjeldbjerg, M. L., & Clausen, L. (2021). Prevalence of binge-eating disorder among children and adolescents: a systematic review and meta-analysis. *European Child & Adolescent Psychiatry, 32*(4), 549–574. https://doi.org/10.1007/s00787-021-01850-2

Kronengold, C. (2016, November 30). *Unpacking the Term "Binge Eating Disorder."* National Eating Disorders Association. https://www.nationaleatingdisorders.org/blog/unpacking-term-binge-eating-disorder

Linardon, J. (2018). Rates of abstinence following psychological or behavioral treatments for binge-eating disorder: Meta-analysis. *International Journal of Eating Disorders, 51*(8), 785–797. https://doi.org/10.1002/eat.22897

Linardon, J., Rosato, J., & Messer, M. (2020). Break Binge Eating: Reach, engagement, and user profile of an Internet-based psychoeducational and self-help platform for eating disorders. *International Journal of Eating Disorders, 53*, 1719–1728.

López-Gil, J. F., García-Hermoso, A., Smith, L., Firth, J., Trott, M., Mesas, A. E., Jiménez-López, E., Gutiérrez-Espinoza, H., Tárraga-López, P. J., & Victoria-Montesinos, D. (2023). Global Proportion of Disordered Eating in Children and Adolescents: A Systematic Review and Meta-analysis. *JAMA Pediatrics, 177*(4). https://doi.org/10.1001/jamapediatrics.2022.5848

Mandl, E. (2019, December 3). *Binge Eating Disorder: Symptoms, Causes, and Treatment.* Healthline. https://www.healthline.com/nutrition/binge-eating-disorder#causes

Martin, R. (2022, January 12). *50 tips for improving your emotional intelligence.* Www.rochemartin.com. https://www.rochemartin.com/blog/50-tips-improving-emotional-intelligence

Marzilli, E., Cerniglia, L., & Cimino, S. (2018). A narrative review of binge eating disorder in adolescence: prevalence, impact, and psychological treatment strategies. *Adolescent Health, Medicine and Therapeutics, Volume 9*, 17–30. https://doi.org/10.2147/ahmt.s148050

Moore, C. (2019, March 4). *Positive Daily Affirmations: Is There Science Behind It?* PositivePsychology.com. https://positivepsychology.com/daily-affirmations/

Morgan, J. (2022, January 12). *How Do We Embrace A Growth Mindset?* Linkedin. https://www.linkedin.com/pulse/how-do-we-embrace-growth-mindset-jacob-morgan?_l=en_US

Muhlheim, L. (2023, January 23). *Body Image and Eating Disorders.* Verywell Mind. https://www.verywellmind.com/body-image-and-eating-disorders-4149424

Murray, S. B., Ganson, K. T., Chu, J., Jann, K., & Nagata, J. M. (2022). The Prevalence of Preadolescent Eating Disorders in the United States. *Journal of Adolescent Health, 70*(5). https://doi.org/10.1016/j.jadohealth.2021.11.031

National Eating Disorders Association. (2018, February 22). *Recovery & Relapse.* National Eating Disorders Association. https://www.nationaleatingdisorders.org/learn/general-information/recovery

National Institute of Mental Health. (2017, November). *Eating Disorders.* National Institute of Mental Health. https://www.nimh.nih.gov/health/statistics/eating-disorders

Nieder, S. (2022, May 11). *Practicing Self-Compassion in Eating Disorder Recovery.* ACUTE. https://www.acute.org/blog/practicing-self-compassion-eating-disorder-recovery

Rehman, A. (2020, June 3). *Eating disorder statistics in the U.S. in 2020.* The Checkup. https://www.singlecare.com/blog/news/eating-disorder-statistics/

Rittenhouse, M. (2020, March 27). *The Art of Self-Compassion in Eating Disorder Recovery.* Eating Disorder Hope. https://www.eatingdisorderhope.com/blog/self-compassion-eating-disorder-recovery

Robinson, L. (2020, October). *Mindful Eating.* HelpGuide.org. https://www.helpguide.org/articles/diets/mindful-eating.htm

Rose, A. (2020, July 13). *Do Not Let Your Mind Bully Your Body.* The Minds Journal. https://themindsjournal.com/quotes/do-not-let-your-mind-bully-your-body/

Rozzell, K., Moon, D. Y., Klimek, P., Brown, T., & Blashill, A. J. (2019). Prevalence of Eating Disorders Among US Children Aged 9 to 10 Years. *JAMA Pediatrics, 173*(1), 100. https://doi.org/10.1001/jamapediatrics.2018.3678

Schaeffer, J. (2015). *Binge Eating Disorder: Statistics, Facts, and You.* Healthline. https://www.healthline.com/health/eating-disorders/binge-eating-disorder-statistics

Seeds of Hope Support. (2022, May 9). *How to Deal with Guilt from Binge Eating.* Seeds of Hope. https://www.seedsofhopesupport.com/6-tips-for-dealing-with-guilt-after-a-binge/

Sheehan, D. V., & Herman, B. K. (2015). The Psychological and Medical Factors Associated With Untreated Binge Eating Disorder. *The Primary Care Companion for CNS Disorders, 17*(2). https://doi.org/10.4088/pcc.14r01732

Sola, A. (2017, December 20). *How Affirmations Can Help in Recovery.* Clear Sky Recovery. https://clearskyibogaine.com/affirmations-can-help-recovery/

Taquet, M., Geddes, J. R., Luciano, S., & Harrison, P. J. (2021). Incidence and outcomes of eating disorders during the COVID-19 pandemic. *The British Journal of Psychiatry, 220*(5), 1–3. https://doi.org/10.1192/bjp.2021.105

The Recovery Village. (2021a, April 14). *Find Out the 7 Myths About Binge Eating Disorder.* The Recovery Village Drug and Alcohol Rehab. https://www.therecoveryvillage.com/mental-health/binge-eating/binge%20eating-myths/

The Recovery Village. (2021b, April 14). *The Relationship Between Binge Eating Disorder and Substance Abuse.* The Recovery Village Drug and Alcohol Rehab. https://www.therecoveryvillage.com/mental-health/binge-eating/substance-abuse/

Turner, C. (2016, March 7). *Understanding, Treating and Coping with Binge Eating Disorder.* National Eating Disorders Association. https://www.nationaleating-disorders.org/blog/understanding-treating-and-coping-binge-eating-disorder

Walen, A. (2016, August 9). *Males Don't Present Like Females with Eating Disorders.* National Eating Disorders Association. https://www.nationaleatingdisorders.org/blog/males-dont-present-females-eating-disorders

Weniger, K. (2022, April 1). *How to Create a Strong Support System: 10 Tips.* Institute for Integrative Nutrition. https://www.integrativenutrition.com/blog/creating-a-strong-support-system

Yamaji, M., Tsutamoto, T., Kawahara, C., Nishiyama, K., Yamamoto, T., Fujii, M., & Horie, M. (2009). Serum Cortisol as a Useful Predictor of Cardiac Events in Patients With Chronic Heart Failure. *Circulation: Heart Failure, 2*(6), 608–615. https://doi.org/10.1161/circheartfailure.109.868513

Printed in Dunstable, United Kingdom

64610938R00105